WHAT READERS ARE
SAYING ABOUT *IMPACT*

Al Etmanski is one of those rare individuals: a leader in social innovation, a system transformer and a thoughtful practitioner; someone who can embed his rich experience in ideas and concepts that give wings to our aspirations. *Impact* will help anyone who longs to make the world a better place take the first step, and the second, and the third. Etmanski is quite simply the best guide we have in that journey of transformation and *Impact* is his Lonely Planet guidebook to social innovation.

— Frances Westley, Author, *Getting to Maybe*

Remember the 'butterfly effect' – how delicate flapping can ripple around the world? *Impact* is the Etmanski effect – a reminder that we have both the opportunity and the responsibility to ACT now on issues that matter in our daily lives. In an era of enormous challenge, this opens a window of hope and possibility. And we can all begin today.

— Jack Pearpoint, President, Inclusion Press

Al Etmanski is wise, smart, and tireless in his practical approach to making the world a better place. This new book, written in plain and compelling prose and full of memorable examples, will help us all become more effective citizens of a planet dominated by the unpredictable economics of attention.

— Mark Kingwell, Professor of Philosophy, University of Toronto

At a time when it seems that societal problems are resistant to change, a set of perspectives and processes linked to the notion of 'social innovation' is enabling us to relate, think and act differently.

Al Etmanski's approach is infused with the spirit of 'bold humility,' and the knowledge that vulnerability and social innovation are inextricably linked.

He shows that when we innovate at the level of pattern as opposed to problem, we are contributing to an essential, evolutionary shift in human culture. I highly recommend *Impact*.

– Stephen Huddart, President and CEO, The J. W. McConnell Family Foundation

Canadians, especially young Canadians, are determined to make our world a better place. Yet, they often do so in the absence of established best practice, often preoccupied with doing as opposed to reflecting. This book is as inspirational as it is practical, and will be extraordinarily helpful to those who strive to bring about significant social change.

– Susan Pigott, Chair, The Change Foundation

Al Etmanski is one of North America's greatest social inventors, and that's reason enough to read this book. It is a chronicle of the wisdom he has gained in exploring the keys to long-term social change. His findings lead us out of the past and onto a pathway for progress in the 21st century.

– John McKnight, Co-Director Asset Based Community
Development Institute, Northwestern University

Anyone involved in the heady and confounding business of mending the world will find tremendous practical value in these pages. More importantly, they will be invited to explore the spiritual dimension of their work and embark on the personal journey that is a necessary prelude to inspiring change in the world around us.

– Liz Mulholland, CEO, Prosper Canada

Our social and environmental problems cannot be solved by technology or industry but by dialogue and cooperation, new types of human relations, new social organizations, and new public policies and programs. In this book, Al Etmanski explains simply and clearly how to do it. *Impact* must be read and then applied.

— Michel Venne, Founder and Executive Director, Institut du Nouveau Monde

Al leads us through a journey of learning and insight with humility and passion. He grounds us in the limits of reality as well as the hope to dream and create big change.

— Tatiana Fraser, Co-Founder, Girls Action Foundation

This is an important book for anyone who aspires to make their community or country a better place to live. It will remind you how much power we all have to make a difference.

— Alison Loat, Co-founder and Executive Director, Samara

I have been awaiting the arrival of another great book on social innovation ever since *Getting to Maybe*. *Impact* is it.

Impact explores the underlying rules of developing deeper, broader and more durable solutions to complex challenges. It is wise, humble, enlightening, and a great read. This is an important book for anyone committed to building a better world.

— Mark Cabaj, President, Here to There

Impact captures the frustrations changemakers feel when they know they are onto to something powerful and possibly impactful if only…

— Allyson Hewitt, SiG@MaRS

This work is delicious brain and heart food for those on the journey of social change. *Impact* makes for an easy and inspiring read.

— Ken Gauthier, Founder and President, Urban Matters CCC,
Co-Chair, BC Partners for Social Impact

Etmanski reminds us that we all have a role to play in social change if we pay attention to the right signals and invest in the right habits. *Impact* will help many people connect the dots in a practical and accessible manner.

— Anil Patel, Managing Director, Digital Strategy, Grant Book

Etmanski, drawing upon his rich experiences in the disability community and beyond, identifies the principles and patterns that we must adopt to become powerful and effective social innovators. With his methods we can move our ideas from the margins to the mainstream and add our contributions to making the world a better place.

— Ted Kuntz, Chair, PLAN and Author, *Peace Begins With Me*

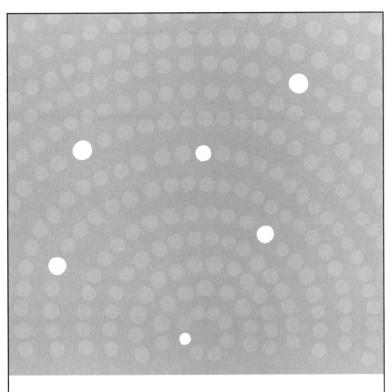

IMPACT

SIX PATTERNS TO SPREAD YOUR SOCIAL INNOVATION

Al Etmanski

Foreword: Severn Cullis-Suzuki
Prologue: Vickie Cammack

© Copyright 2015 Al Etmanski

First Edition – March, 2015
Orwell Cove

Feel free to circulate excerpts of *Impact* for non-commercial purposes. I'd appreciate acknowledgement where appropriate and that you encourage people to subscribe to my blog .
www.aletmanski.com

BOOK COVER AND DESIGN Sara Bailey, Mika Creative

EDITORIAL TEAM
Barbara Pulling
Frances Peck
Linda McDaniel

PRODUCTION www.workingdesign.net

ISBN 978-0-9680462-3-4 (pbk.)
ISBN 978-0-9680462-4-1 (audio)
ISBN 978-0-9680462-5-8 (epub)

Library and Archives Canada Cataloguing in Publication

Etmanski, Al, 1947-, author

IMPACT – six patterns to spread your social innovation
/ Al Etmanski.

1. Social action. 2. Social advocacy. 3. Social justice. I. Title

HM831.E85 2015   303.4   C2015-900366-0

TYPESET IN Neutraface Text, Whitney & Garamond Pro

PRINTED IN Canada

This book is printed on stock that is acid-free, FSC Certified and ethically sourced.

DEDICATION

To Jack Collins and his daughter Pam, Joan Lawrence and her son Keith, Chuck Walker and his son Gordon – true passionate amateurs.

TABLE OF CONTENTS

FOREWORD

How can we change the world?

This is something I've asked my whole life. Maybe I've been asking this because I saw it happen once, when I was a child. It was in the 1980s, when the world was watching events unfold on Haida Gwaii, the island chain of the Haida people off the coast of BC. Like many other Canadians, my parents joined in to support the Haida Nation to save South Moresby, a national treasure of old growth rainforest, from clearcut logging. Elders were arrested for blockading logging trucks, loggers fought for jobs, scores of Haida people were taken to court, and grassroots environmentalists organized on the mainland to grow public support.

Somehow it grew into a national cause, then a global one – an iconic struggle for indigenous sovereignty and forests versus economic interests. Incredibly, the provincial and federal governments aligned with the Haida and protected the southern third of the Haida Gwaii. This area would become the Gwaii Haanas National Park Reserve, co-managed by the Haida Nation and the Government of Canada in a landmark agreement.

Today Gwaii Haanas is a sacred place for Haidas as well as non-Haida locals and visitors, and the National Park Reserve is an important employer and political force on the islands. Even the maps have been officially corrected to Haida Gwaii returning the old name, the Queen Charlotte Islands, back to Canada.

The world was indeed changed.

The experience to save South Moresby was pivotal for all who were part of it. It was a compelling and magical time when people were united and the impossible became reality. After that, even though I was just a kid, I got involved in environmental and indigenous issues, starting a club and advocating for intergenerational justice. My parents founded and painstakingly grew their non-profit environmental foundation. I recognize we are the 'passionate amateurs' that Al talks about in *Impact*.

Decades after the height of environmentalism, there are now several large environmental non-governmental organizations in Canada. But while the budgets of our organizations and our professionalism have grown, so too have the problems. We have done a lot, our list of accomplishments are long, but the challenges loom larger than ever. I now have children of my own, yet the problems my parents fought to solve remain. Hard won environmental legislation has been reversed. Mining, fracking and pipeline proposals overwhelm small communities. And our climate is changing all around us. Gwaii Haanas is one of only a few examples of successful, profound change.

My question has changed from 'how can I change the world,' to 'why isn't it working?' Many activists are asking this. We need to take stock. We have not succeeded in bringing justice, equity and sustainability, and we need to assess what we are doing. We need a meta-analysis of how to create conditions for success.

When I read *Impact*, I was amazed to find someone not only tackling this question, but transforming the critique into a positive offering of solutions. The analysis in *Impact* shares practical patterns and conditions that foster social innovation and transformation, with a systems approach, derived from Al's work and research. But the instruction is delivered with deep empathy for those trying to make a difference; it comes from a person who has spent his life working toward social change out of necessity and out of love. The compassion and reflection embedded in the identified principles is very moving. If Al's six patterns become the means, then they will certainly justify the ends.

I now live on Haida Gwaii. My husband works for the Gwaii Haanas National Park Reserve. We have two children who have inherited the privilege and responsibility of being Haida, living on the islands, and being residents of Planet Earth in the 21st century. We are the product of many of the patterns that were at play when the fight for South Moresby moved beyond struggle and became collaboration. Thinking back on that heady time, it seemed magical how people unified, reached out and worked to find solutions together. Reading *Impact*, I can see that the magic was in the patterns and the optimal conditions for social innovation and change.

Let's bring magic into our work. Al has learned through his successes and failures that coming together is the only way forward. We are not alone; we are inextricably dependent on one another, and that's what is so difficult and so beautiful. It is my hope that those of us trying to positively change this world can take stock and figure out how to bring magic to our movements. This book will help us do that. Then we can begin to foster the conditions that will create real and permanent progress for the next generation.

Severn Cullis-Suzuki
Skidegate, Haida Gwaii
severncullissuzuki.com

PROLOGUE

This book is a journey.

Al and I knew our good work wasn't good enough. Ten years ago, facing that cold reality, we began our social innovation journey.

We could sense in our bones the deep change that was needed – a cultural shift from needs and inability to capacity and contribution. But this seemed wild and impossible to imagine, arrogant even, and certainly not achievable in our lifetime. Called by the light of a distant north star to think bigger and act bolder than we thought we could, we set off without a road, path or map… quaking in our boots.

This book is a guide.

Conversations. Reflections. Rebuttals. Distillations. These daily acts helped us feel our way, touching ley lines and finding the patterns that form the backbone of *Impact*. The stories, actions, programs and initiatives and most importantly the innovators behind them nourished us. We were intellectually stretched and profoundly inspired. Turns out the journey can teach you a lot about the destination.

This book is a gift.

Energized and emboldened, a few years back our paths to our shared destination diverged for a time. I dove into social business and technology creating Tyze Personal Networks to further our core work of addressing isolation and fostering belonging. Al dove into the world of social innovation, exploring and testing new insights and vistas. He nurtured generative partnerships and collaborations that set a new bar for working across differences to achieve social change.

Each step on our common and separate paths has informed the other's, layering learning upon learning. In this book Al has made beautiful sense of our wanderings. But he does so much more. He stretches and inspires us and holds up the mirror so we can each find ourselves in its pages. I am filled with gratitude for it.

And so our journey continues…

With love,
Vickie Cammack

INTRODUCTION

The future is already here – it's just not very evenly distributed.

– William Gibson, National Public Radio interview

Do you want to change the world but feel frustrated by the limited impact you and others have had? Do you feel that despite your best efforts, and indeed successes, you have hit a brick wall? You may have mounted a fierce advocacy campaign, seen your public education campaign go viral, pioneered a social program, mobilized new funds or changed a law, but the status quo has barely budged. Social and economic justice hasn't increased. Power hasn't shifted. The old paradigm survives. And the sharp, distinctive edges of your social innovation are in danger of being eroded, isolated or forgotten.

The paradox of short-term success versus long-term impact is the central question this book addresses. Many of us believed that by now we would have absolute poverty under control. Or pollution. Or child abuse. Or deforestation. Or any number of other social and environmental challenges. The solutions certainly exist. They just aren't widely distributed.

Why do some social innovations take hold while others don't spread as far and wide as they should? Consider Women's Institutes, described by the Young Foundation as one of the top ten social innovations in the world. The first Women's Institute was founded in 1897 by Adelaide Hoodless in Stoney Creek, Ontario, in response to children dying because of poor hygienic practices in food production. Today Women's Institutes have a combined membership of nine million women from more than seventy countries and are credited with launching the first wave of feminism. It's a Canadian irony that the Women's Institute is better known in the UK than in Canada. The 2003 British film *Calendar Girls*, for example, is a fictionalized account of a real group from a

Yorkshire Women's Institute who raised money for cancer research by posing nude for a calendar.

Another social innovation that has taken hold is microcredit, pioneered by Muhammad Yunus. The Grameen Bank he created has provided over $5 billion in small loans to 5.6 million borrowers, primarily women, in rural Bangladesh. Today more than 250 institutions in nearly 100 countries operate microcredit programs based on the Grameen Bank model. In addition, thousands of other microcredit programs have emulated, adapted or been inspired by the Grameen Bank, benefiting over 80 million people worldwide. One expert in innovative government has called the Grameen Bank program "the single most important development in the third world in the last 100 years."

A third example is Greenpeace. Founded in 1971 in my home city of Vancouver, a small group of activists set sail for Amchitka, Alaska, to protest nuclear testing. The organization now has nearly three million members worldwide and a bigger budget than most countries spend on environmental issues. Greenpeace invented modern environmental activism by straddling national boundaries and catching the world's imagination with its media "mind bombs," a term Greenpeace co-founder Bob Hunter used to describe actions that dispense with old clichés to create dramatic new impressions of an issue.

That's the kind of impact we all want.

What gave these groups the momentum not only to change laws and funding priorities but also to shift popular beliefs and the way we do things? How did they reach beyond the converted? How did they survive, indeed thrive, despite the odds against them?

These questions have plagued and fascinated me ever since I realized that lasting impact requires more than coming up with a new idea and proving that it works.

Novelty isn't enough. Neither are dedication and hard work, or loyal supporters, or a sophisticated strategy, or money.

Are these things essential? Yes. A good start? Certainly. But not enough to tip a system.

Just because you have a shiny new solution, the world will not beat a path to your door. Enduring social innovation doesn't spread by accident. We need to deliberately nurture the conditions in which it can flourish.

****

That's not an easy lesson to learn, and it's one I confess I'm still learning. I've spent most of my adult life as a community organizer, starting as an adult educator with Frontier College in an asbestos mine in Cassiar, British Columbia. I was a youth worker on the streets of Halifax and a social housing planner in Vancouver.

When my second daughter was born with Down syndrome, I became a parent activist in the disability movement. My anger and righteousness had finally found a home. "Nurture" wasn't part of my vocabulary. My allusions and metaphors were all drawn from the military. My advocacy was fuelled as much by the chip on my shoulder as by a desire for justice.

I soon became head of the largest disability rights group in BC. Our activism produced a string of successes, including the closure of BC's three large institutions for people with developmental disabilities, all its segregated schools and many of its segregated classrooms and sheltered workshops. We blocked roads, sued government and won an important right-to-treatment court case. This all gave birth to what is now called the community living movement.

For me, these advances were tarnished by two realizations, one personal and the other cultural. First, my warrior mentality had taken its toll. I had become the very dragon I'd set out to slay. I left behind me a trail of busted relationships, particularly with government but also with some of my colleagues. Second, although the physical institutions were closing, an institutional mentality still occupied society's collective psyche. People with disabilities were no longer segregated, but they were not part of their communities.

Pity, charity and low expectations dominated. Society neither recognized people with disabilities nor expected them to become contributing members of society. My take-no-prisoners style may have removed one set of challenges, but it wasn't sufficient to tackle the next set, and I had fewer allies than opponents left to rely on.

Fortunately, I was given the chance to try another way when a group of older parents posed the question: "What's going to happen to our sons and daughters with disabilities when we die?"

By then I had become partners in life as well as in work with Vickie Cammack. Vickie was the founding director of Canada's first Family Support Institute, and she had launched a series of innovations in family support. She and I agreed to work with these older parents on what we thought would be a short-term project that would benefit a few dozen families.

To our surprise, we encountered a demographic tsunami. For the first time in history, a generation of people with disabilities was about to outlive their parents, and no one was doing anything about it. The situation wasn't on the radar of government, service providers or even most parents.

In 1989 Vickie and I and these families created Planned Lifetime Advocacy Network (PLAN). In doing so, we adopted a mindset and a mandate unlike those of any other disability organization. We knew we had to rethink the whole approach to disability. We realized that one of the biggest handicaps facing people with disabilities was their social isolation. PLAN believed that if this challenge could be addressed, parents would have an answer to their worries about the future. That's why we specialized in developing personal networks of support for people with disabilities well before the term "network" had entered the zeitgeist.

Fifteen years after PLAN was established, the dilemma of short-term success versus long-term impact became an existential crisis for Vickie and me.

By most measures PLAN was successful. Groups of families were adapting our model in other parts of Canada, Europe,

Australia, New Zealand and the US. PLAN had garnered much media attention. It was even the subject of three public education spots aired during the last episode of Seinfeld, which everyone in North America seemed to watch.

The scramble for organizational security appeared to be over. Foundations wanted to fund us. Vickie and I had received numerous awards and accolades. Enthusiasm, passion and momentum were everywhere. We should have been enjoying ourselves.

Instead, we were disheartened. Vickie and I were losing confidence that PLAN or its replications would ever make a dent in the profound loneliness experienced by people with disabilities. No matter how hard we worked, it seemed to us that this goal would take several lifetimes to accomplish.

We weren't sure what to do. We were so out of step with everyone else in the PLAN family that we felt like frauds. We loved PLAN, but we wondered if we should leave.

At the same time Vickie and I were struggling with our limitations, we were given a dream assignment by Tim Brodhead, then president and CEO of the J. W. McConnell Family Foundation. One of Canada's largest and most progressive private foundations, the McConnell Foundation had funded PLAN's replication strategy, and we had come to know Tim quite well. Tim's dilemma was similar to ours. The foundation funded a number of successful organizations across Canada, but neither Tim nor the organizations were satisfied with the impact they were having. In some cases, their intervention had made no difference to the overall statistics. In others, the problem had actually become worse.

Tim believed that people were trying to meet twenty-first-century challenges with institutions, funding methods and policies largely fashioned in and for the twentieth century. He felt it was time for fresh thinking. He wondered if there was a better way to effect social change, and he asked Vickie and me to explore the emerging field of social innovation for insight and practical applications.

From 2004 to 2006 Vickie and I dove into the burgeoning literature on social innovation. We travelled across North America meeting activists, social entrepreneurs, thinkers, philanthropists, businesspeople and policy makers. And there, amid the swirl of ideas and inspiration, we discovered six deep patterns being used to successfully escort social innovations from the margins to the mainstream.

This book highlights those six patterns while tracing the insights we gained on our two-year journey – and our continuous learning since then.

Social Innovation and Impact

Social innovation is the latest descriptor of the ageless human pursuit to make the world a better place. It is a bundle of new learning, technologies and methods blended with the best traditional approaches to social change.

In this book and in my ongoing work, I'm less interested in defining social innovation than in clarifying its intent. Social innovation is an opportunity to renew the focus on social change. We have to stop doing things in the same way if we want to get different results. When applied thoughtfully, social innovation ideas and methods can become the catalyst for a renaissance in social problem solving. They can help us address the roots of an issue, not just the symptoms.

Humans' ingenuity and creativity in the face of adversity define us as a species. In that regard social innovation is not new. What is new is the recognition that many of our toughest social and environmental challenges have had time to develop deep roots that are resistant to just about everything we throw at them. Furthermore, these roots are intertwined with related problems that are just as entrenched. Think, for example, of the connections between homelessness, poverty, hunger, addiction, mental illness, discrimination and social isolation. Each challenge is complex enough on its own. Together, they are impossible for any one individual, group, institution or sector to tackle.

If we are to be innovative about anything in the future, it must be about how we work together. Yes, social innovators have to be dedicated and creative problem solvers. But they also have to be wise travellers. Social innovation spreads through sharing, not selfishness. The heroic "great man" model of social change makes for a good story, but it isn't true in practice. It is only through generous, respectful interactions across sectors, expertise and roles that social innovation achieves lasting impact.

That's why of all the definitions of social innovation I've seen, I like Tim Brodhead's the best:

> Social innovation is both a destination – the resolution of complex social and environmental challenges – and a journey – devising new approaches that engage all stakeholders, leveraging their competencies and creativity to design novel solutions.

Pattern Recognition

Change is composed of more unknown than known variables, accompanied by a dash of surprise. You may be certain of the general direction in which you're headed, but the precise destination often reveals itself only once you begin.

In the early days of PLAN, for example, we thought the best solution for the future well-being of people with disabilities was to encourage parents to develop a will and an estate plan. Nice and concrete, and very tangible. Then we realized that neither a well-written will nor a decent-sized estate could deliver what parents really wanted: someone to love their son or daughter when they themselves were gone. This led to the realization that, aside from their parents, most people with disabilities had no friends. This in turn informed PLAN's decision to specialize in developing caring networks made up of friends and family.

It's useful to have a strategic plan. It gets you started. But if you become too fixated on predetermined goals, you may not see what's actually happening. When something out of the ordinary occurs, you may view it as random or irrelevant. You may not appreciate its deeper significance.

"[W]hat pattern," asked Gregory Bateson, a key figure in systems theory, "connects the crab to the lobster and the orchid to the primrose and all the four of them to me? And me to you?" There is no such thing as something that is separate from something else. Insight emerges when you connect the dots and recognize an underlying pattern.

Pattern recognition will also help you become more deliberate and intentional about your actions. It will help you to anticipate and to discern, revealing meaning in seemingly random or irrelevant events. As the authors of *Getting to Maybe* point out, recognizing patterns helps you uncover "obstacles, accelerants, traps or enablers" and spot "strange bedfellows" and "powerful strangers." Every groove eventually becomes a rut. We have to become as smart and conscious about pattern recognition as we are about everything else.

A pattern is not just something you can train yourself to observe – it's also something you can follow. A pattern is a codified collection of insights, lessons, relationships, stories, values and desires you can apply directly to your work. That's the sense in which I use the word in this book.

Six Patterns to Achieve Impact

In our encounters with dozens of individuals, groups, coalitions and movements during our social innovation exploration, Vickie and I discovered six patterns that stood out. These patterns challenged our thinking and forced us to let go of many of our certainties about social change. They were our doorways into pattern recognition. And once we understood the underlying significance of these approaches, our own work changed profoundly.

The six patterns I present in this book do not exist independently of each other. Rather, they are mutually reinforcing, blending, merging and overlapping in various ways. Here they are in brief.

Pattern One: Think and Act like a Movement

This pattern is not about starting a movement, although your actions may be the spark that ignites one. Instead, it's about supporting the movement(s) you are already part of. That means paying attention to the key players and initiatives in your immediate field and beyond, and becoming more deliberate about aligning your efforts. When you think and act like a movement, you strengthen the specific work you are doing and expand general receptivity for the bold vision behind it.

Pattern Two: Create a Container for Your Content

This pattern invites you to do more than come up with the right analysis or solution. You also have to make it easy for people to do the right thing. Otherwise, there's too much for them to digest. You must create a literal or figurative container for your vision, data and values in a way that makes your message easy to grasp. Content is essential, but framing and packaging will enliven your ideas and inspire people to action.

Pattern Three: Set the Table for Allies, Adversaries and Strangers

You and others won't achieve lasting impact as long as you work on parallel tracks or at loggerheads. Changing that situation requires more than the usual suspects to be at the table. Dialogue and convening are more than a means to an end. They give structure to our need to belong, to be part of something bigger than ourselves. They broaden understanding, puncture assumptions, change authority flows and allow us to cultivate new relationships. Solutions spread when we move beyond blame, competition, misunderstanding and mistrust.

Pattern Four: Mobilize Your Economic Power

Your membership or constituency is an untapped economic market that, when properly mobilized, will both finance and further your social innovation. More and more, social change activists are flexing their economic muscle to disrupt business models, acquire flexible funds, reduce their dependence on grant funding and develop business partnerships that help spread their big ideas.

Pattern Five: Advocate with Empathy

This pattern proposes that we stop poisoning the political ecosystem, put aside tactics of blame and criticism and become solution-based advocates. These advocates have two mutually supportive objectives: they propose solutions and at the same time improve governments' capacity to innovate. Regardless of their political stripe, today's governments have shorter attention spans and are more risk-averse. It's no wonder new policy ideas fight for a foothold. If we want government to have empathy for our issues, we must develop empathy for its issues as well.

Pattern Six: Who Is as Important as How

An undue focus on how we do social innovation creates the impression that it's a specialty we must be trained for. Instead, social innovation is enlightened by who we are – by character, not technique. The conviction of today's social innovators arises from their emotional and spiritual maturity. They pay attention to what nourishes and replenishes their spirits. And they have the humility to admit their limitations and fears.

How to Use This Book

My hope is that this book will ignite what Pulitzer Prize–winning author Marilynne Robinson describes as a "resurrection of the ordinary." You have an important role in transforming the world. Indeed, without you, it won't happen.

In the book's opening chapter, I stress the importance of being a wise traveller in order for your social innovation to spread.

I pay particular attention to the passionate amateur in each of us, who innovates out of both love and necessity. Then in the chapters that follow, I examine each of the six patterns in more detail. I profile the person who helped me recognize the pattern; identify a few key, underlying concepts; provide a handful of illustrations that demonstrate the pattern in action; and describe how we applied the pattern to our work at PLAN.

I encourage you to treat these patterns as an integrated set rather than applying them piecemeal. Approach them with curiosity. Try them on. Play with them.

Let the patterns wash over you, slowly, thoughtfully and intuitively. Give your imagination free rein. Trust your judgment. Adapt the patterns to your own circumstances. Use them to refresh what you already know.

Most importantly, don't give up too soon. Something will emerge. These patterns have stood the test of time. They are the accumulation of hard-won experiences. When used together, they will increase your chances of achieving impact, durability and scale for your social innovation.

****

Thanks to our two-year exploration of social innovation, Vickie and I found we didn't have to leave PLAN after all. We did, though, hand over the day-to-day running to others and the way we approached our work changed. We had received an advanced course in letting go. Letting go of our beliefs about how to change the world. Letting go of how we worked together. Letting go of how we financed solutions. Letting go of how we approached government. We came away with a deeper understanding about how the world is changing and how to apply these patterns to our work at PLAN and beyond.

We had a few hits and lots of misses. Not all of it was pretty, as you will read. However, playing with these patterns has enabled us to affect the lives of hundreds of thousands rather than hundreds or thousands. And we've spread our innovations not only within the disability sector but farther and wider than we ever imagined.

May adopting these patterns achieve the same for you.

PLAN – A SOCIAL INNOVATION

Although this is not a book about Planned Lifetime Advocacy Network, my understanding has been informed by the experience Vickie and I had as co-founders. Since you will encounter references to PLAN throughout the book, here is a brief overview for context.

PLAN was founded in 1989 by parents in Vancouver to answer the question: What will happen to our family members with a disability when we die?

Over the years PLAN has been associated with a number of innovations, including these:
- the world's first Registered Disability Savings Plan (RDSP)
- a citizen-based theory of disability
- the representation agreement, a grassroots alternative to legal guardianship
- Tyze Personal Networks, a business started by PLAN to spread the use of caring networks via the web

There are three distinguishing features of PLAN's social innovation.

One, PLAN begins with the question: What is a good life? This is a unifying question for parents. It opens their hearts, minds and imaginations regardless of circumstances, age, beliefs or life experience. Discussions about a good life get to the core of every family's hopes, dreams, worries and fears for their relative with a disability. It invites them to think beyond reliance on professional services to important considerations like friends and family, financial security and a meaningful life.

Two, PLAN is a social enterprise. We don't rely on government grants for our operations. Instead, we earn our income by selling our intellectual and social capital. We charge a fee for some of our products and services to those who can afford it. We seek partnerships with financial institutions, law firms, trust companies and estate-planning specialists. We also have a successful publishing arm and started the private business Tyze.

Earning our own revenue gives us flexible funding and independence. We can champion issues that benefit the financial and social well-being of people with disabilities and their families without fear of consequence.

Three, PLAN operates from a citizenship paradigm. We know that people with disabilities have an important contribution to make to society. They are an underestimated and underutilized resource. PLAN families want to replace notions of pity and charity with the expectation that people with disabilities, like all citizens, have a responsibility to contribute their gifts.

WISE TRAVELLERS: THE SOCIAL INNOVATOR'S JOURNEY

Then, when he had flown a while longer,
something brightened toward the north.
It caught his eye, they say.
And then he flew right up against it.

He pushed his mind through
and pulled his body after.

— Skaay, "Raven Travelling"

"We're going to die, and we're afraid." It wasn't the kind of idle chatter I'd expected at a Christmas party.

In the 1980s I was head of the British Columbia Association for Community Living (BCACL), the largest disability organization in BC. We had successfully campaigned for the closure of institutions and segregated "special" schools for people with developmental disabilities, as well as for inclusion in society. We had a robust advocacy agenda, and I thought we had everything covered – until two worried dads took me aside at our annual open house and confided, "We're pleased with the inroads BCACL is making, but it's not going to be of much help to us."

"What do you mean?" I asked, having trouble imagining any gaps in our strategic plan.

"Well, young fella, we're facing something you won't have to for a while," said Chuck, one of the dads. "We're going to die sooner rather than later. And when we look around, we don't see the kind of supports my son and Jack's daughter will need when we're gone. We're afraid. Will you help us?"

Those two fathers had put their finger on a brand new social challenge. Thanks to medical advances and social inclusion, the son and daughter of these parents, and hundreds of thousands like them, would soon become the first generation of people with disabilities to outlive their parents. Yet policies, priorities and systems of support had been designed on the outdated assumption that the majority of people with disabilities would die before their parents. Not only were there scarce resources to respond to this looming challenge, but policy makers, funders, service providers and advocates like me hadn't been aware of it. We would soon discover that this was a global concern.

Most tellingly, those parents recognized that existing services and programs did not answer the question closest to their heart: Who will love my child when I die? Even though both fathers had spent much of their lives helping develop the disability service system, they knew it was no longer enough. They were willing to let go of what they'd once believed so that they could explore. They had what is now called an innovator's mindset. Within a year of this conversation, PLAN was founded.

You know more than you think you do about social innovation.

Those two dads did. So do the thousands of PLAN families we've met around the world over the past twenty-five years. So does everyone.

The capacity to innovate is a human trait. Our ingenuity when faced with a predicament defines us as a species. It's an aspect of ourselves we can count on, not a specialty reserved for a few. So-called ordinary people are constantly inventing solutions most of us can't yet see. Our job is to tap into this latent force in ourselves and in others.

This chapter's opening stanza comes from Skaay, an oral poet from Haida Gwaii, a group of islands off the northwest coast of British Columbia. Skaay, whom many consider to be Canada's Homer, makes it clear that the social innovator's journey starts with a change in thinking.

Something's not working. Injustice burns bright. A possibility catches your eye. Your imagination takes hold. You set aside prevailing wisdom and the way it's supposed to be. With few resources and no one listening, you persist. You answer "yes!" to the uninterested, the doubters and the disbelievers. You take a leap. You strike out. You push your mind through.

You know we can do better. You create a solution to a problem faced by a family member, a friend, a neighbour, a species, a region or the planet. You come up with a successful response to a social or environmental challenge. You improve how people work together. You leverage limited financial resources to attract new sources of funding and investment. You see a new way for your community, your region, your country and your world to be a better place.

You are, in today's parlance, a social innovator.

Social innovation gives us the opportunity to ignite a renaissance of social problem solving. It's the current descriptor of the myriad ways people are concentrating their creative efforts to address the tough challenges of our times. Social innovation integrates the best of the community sector's traditional creativity with new insights about how to address complex problems. And it always begins with what you care deeply about.

Passionate Amateurs: The Sacred Headwaters of Social Innovation

In *The Sacred Headwaters*, author Wade Davis describes a wonder of British Columbia geography: the valley that's home to the headwaters of Canada's most important salmon rivers – the Stikine, the Skeena and the Nass – as well as the origins of the great Mackenzie River. Owing to its bountiful wildlife, the region is known as the Serengeti of Canada. Here among the mountains, glaciers, impassable canyons and alpine meadows, the water is pure and life-giving.

Similarly, there exists a bountiful source of social innovation: the individuals, families, neighbours and so-called ordinary citizens who are constantly working to make things better. Many of their ideas eventually migrate to the nonprofit, business and public sectors. Some of their ideas are destined to become our new institutions. The British author and social innovator Charles Leadbeater was the first to describe these people as passionate amateurs.

Passionate amateurs inhabit the sacred headwaters of social innovation.

Adelaide Hoodless, founder of the first Women's Institute, was a passionate amateur. She was moved to action after the tragic death in 1889 of her infant son, Jack, from drinking contaminated milk. The passionate amateurs behind the slow food movement are farmers, cooks and consumers who want to halt the spread of fast-food restaurants and to preserve centuries-old traditions of producing and enjoying food. Many other widespread social innovations came from passionate amateurs: Alcoholics Anonymous, hospice care, microcredit, carpooling and couchsurfing are just a few examples.

The cross-cultural anthropologist Angeles Arrien believed that when you boil it down, there are only two purposes to being human: to love and to create. I agree. If necessity is the mother of invention, then love is the other parent. Passionate amateurs are motivated by necessity and inspired by love. Someone or something they care about is vulnerable, under siege or in trouble, and they have no choice but to respond.

Passionate amateurs don't quit. They can't quit. They are prepared to pour their life's energy into resolving a challenge. Their commitment is freely given, beyond the boundaries of job descriptions, office hours, strategic plans, funding and political priorities. They are on the front lines, spotting and dealing with injustice years and sometimes decades before the issue seeps into the consciousness of organizations and institutions. Their actions are expressions of the heart.

It's essential to pay attention to what passionate amateurs come up with. Their working conditions are optimal for breakthroughs. They experience or witness the barriers and system failures first-hand. Their intention is unwavering. Their standards are high. They know that slow, incremental change isn't good enough for the people, places and creatures they love.

What's more, their creative skills deepen over time. Their social innovations are the result of repeated failures, of continual attempts to make things better. Their resources are limited, so they know how to stretch a dollar and make the best use of whatever materials are at hand.

Wise Travellers: The Three Types of Social Innovators

The solutions developed by passionate amateurs realize their full potential when people work together: first by joining with others who experience the same challenge, and ultimately by teaming up with nonprofits, businesses and government.

I'm old enough to remember seeing the odd notice on an office bulletin board asking if anyone wanted to share a ride to work. Eventually, there were enough of us to establish small car co-ops. Today there are car-sharing co-ops across Canada as well as commercial alternatives. Furthermore, governments now set aside highway lanes for vehicles with multiple riders. These are all examples of the variety of players needed to spread a good idea.

PLAN's campaign for what eventually became Canada's Registered Disability Savings Plan evolved in the same way. The impetus came from families who wanted to reduce the poverty experienced by their relatives with disabilities. They wanted a way to financially support their relatives without jeopardizing existing government benefits. Many families felt trapped by a welfare system that didn't allow them to build a nest egg for their relatives.

PLAN's original proposal was akin to a huge, rough, flawed piece of marble. We could see some kind of disability savings plan in the marble. At first it was fused with two other components, a pooled investment trust and what we called a "no one alone" fund. We couldn't imagine any of the three proceeding without the other two. Yet our bulky three-pronged proposal confused everyone. We spent years trying to explain our grand idea.

We were going nowhere until we learned the truth of the thinking behind a quote that I found in the Waterloo Region Museum's exhibit *Unconventional Thinking*: "A new idea is fragile. Its success depends upon the environment in which it emerges." We started to pay attention to all the players in the environment surrounding our idea: those who would use it as well as those who would finance, promote and implement it. The momentum shifted, and in 2008 the world's first RDSP became a reality.

Today there are more than two billion RDSP dollars in the bank accounts of people with disabilities. That money doesn't affect their eligibility for government benefits. It can't be clawed back, and there are no restrictions on what the money can be spent on. PLAN estimates the eventual RDSP market will be $12 billion, affecting 700,000 Canadians with disabilities and their families.

Wise travellers know their boundaries. We can only go so far on our own. Social innovations will remain marginalized and isolated unless both the people and the systems surrounding them are engaged.

Three types of social innovators – disruptive, bridging and receptive – are required to achieve long-term impact. While each group has its own set of skills, strengths and limitations, they all have one thing in common: they understand the boundaries of their expertise and experience, and welcome fellow travellers from organizations and institutions that have complementary skills.

1. Disruptive Innovators

Passionate amateurs are the original disruptive innovators. They challenge the prevailing way of doing things – the allocation of resources, the power and advice of professionals, and the very purpose of a policy, program or organization. They shake the lethargy off the status quo. They wrestle a big idea to the ground and make it concrete, with limited resources. They prove that the idea works.

Disruptive possibilities are found in the most surprising places. In every community, no matter how small or remote, there are people meeting in living rooms and coffee shops, scribbling at their kitchen tables and on their laptops, as they develop ideas for addressing their common challenges. Countless people devote their spare time to making the world a better place. John McKnight and Peter Block, authors of *Abundant Community*, express it this way: "Each neighborhood has people with the gifts and talents needed to provide for our prosperity and peace of mind...."

Yet new models, no matter how successful, do not easily become the new standard. They can be ignored or misunderstood. They may be perceived as a threat to the system, inviting hostility or ridicule. It's not easy to move a new idea from the margins to the mainstream. That's why bridging innovators are essential.

2. Bridging Innovators

Bridging innovators are the link between disruptive innovators and formal organizations and institutions. Bridging innovators excel at spotting the potential in big ideas, then leveraging their connections, reputations and resources to make sure that potential is realized. Their support makes disruptive innovators more credible to others in the system. They are equally sympathetic to the struggles of originators and the restraints of institutions. They act as broker, coach, buffer, champion, liaison and sometimes peacemaker.

These intermediaries explain to disruptors how best to describe or package an idea so it can be understood. They also interpret for disruptors the constraints, subtleties and openings in the system. Foundations, for example, are great bridging innovators. They are well connected, have convening power and offer funds to help you work out the kinks in your idea. Alan Broadbent, chairman of the Maytree Foundation, looked at PLAN's three-pronged proposal for the disability savings plan and gave us blunt advice: "Choose one and park the other two." Fortunately, we made the right choice. The reaction shifted from "I don't understand" to "This is common sense. Why haven't we done this before?"

On the other side of the equation, bridging innovators help people inside institutions to understand the implications and benefits of the proposed innovation. Sherri Torjman from the Caledon Institute of Social Policy played this role for PLAN. At the time, Sherri chaired the Technical Advisory Committee on Tax Measures for Persons with Disabilities for the federal government. She introduced us to Keith Horner, a recently retired senior public servant from the federal Department of Finance. Keith's expertise was in registered retirement savings plans. Thanks to Sherri's connection, we hired him to calculate the estimated costs of a disability savings plan. Keith estimated that each tax dollar from government would attract another three dollars from families. Based on credible evidence from one of their own, Department of Finance officials finally started to take us seriously.

3. Receptive Innovators

Bridging innovators act as the link between disruptive innovators and receptive innovators. Disruptive innovators who want to see their solutions widely adopted will eventually rub shoulders with society's institutions. Inevitably, there will be some sort of handover in the form of a new law, pool of funds or regulation. Receptive innovators are the ones with the expertise to get it done. Some people describe receptive innovators as institutional entrepreneurs or "intra-preneurs." Essentially, they are talented and committed bureaucrats.

Author and academic Frances Westley, in a paper she co-wrote with Michele-Lee Moore, describes the job of receptive innovators as managing "the context, complex as it is, in such a way that the innovation has a chance to flourish, widening the circle of its impact." Receptive innovators have an insider's knowledge of the key levers needed to advance an issue, as well as when to move them. They are navigators, steering the innovation so that it may flourish and become the new standard. Their specialty is reorganizing their institutions to make sure the solution takes hold the way it was intended rather than being watered down.

Less than eighteen months after the RDSP was approved in principle, public servants in two federal departments and thirteen provincial and territorial bureaucracies had turned traditional welfare systems on their heads; they created new procedures for the world's first registered financial product for people with disabilities by removing asset limits and eliminating clawbacks. Over the same period, financial institutions put together the infrastructure that now makes it possible for Canadians with disabilities to establish an RDSP in nearly every bank and credit union in Canada. Those are big systems to turn around, and it was all done in record time. The process required expertise and resources that went beyond PLAN's capacity, expertise or role.

Typically, receptive innovators remain anonymous, working competently behind the scenes. Since they are part of large bureaucracies that eschew flamboyancy, they may not be easy to spot. They are there, however, and they are as talented, committed and essential as any other social innovator. They are also proof that social innovators don't have a dress code.

****

These three social innovation roles are not discrete. Some individuals and organizations play more than one role. Receptive innovators, for example, are in effect disruptive innovators within systems. Foundations can become disruptors too, although it can be awkward when their representatives sit down at the table with people the foundation is funding or could potentially fund. Disruptive innovators often become bridge builders as well. Vickie and I have certainly found ourselves taking off our disruptor hats and playing a bridging role to advance PLAN's innovations.

In reality, there is a passionate amateur in each of us. Whatever part we play, our effectiveness improves when we fall in love with the issue – its mystery, its brokenness, its contradictions. Without that love, we're more likely to walk away from an innovation, to give up or get distracted. Tapping into our experiences as passionate amateurs allows us to participate wholeheartedly. One reason an initiative doesn't succeed is that there aren't enough people falling in love with it. Or we haven't found a way to tie in with what people care deeply about. The necessity to do something is usually clear. The challenge is to bring necessity together with love.

There is one caveat to the interdependence between disruptive, bridging and receptive innovators. Disruptive innovators often aren't organized into a group. These individuals are not a definable sector like nonprofits, government or business. As a result, they may be overlooked or excluded from the social innovation journey. Inadvertently, perhaps, disruptive innovators are often denied the chance to share their expertise directly. Ensuring their presence and participation from start to finish will preserve the purity and intent of their original invention. In the end, disruptors' diverse viewpoints and original perspectives strengthen everyone's innovative capacity. A good working slogan adapted from the disability movement is "Nothing about them, without them."

Conclusion

Spoken-word artist Shane Koyczan ends his poem "Tarot" with this line: "The fool steps blindly, reminding us we cannot simply bear what is necessary, we must love it."

There are many reasons for making things better, but the most powerful and enduring social innovations emerge when someone or something we care deeply about is vulnerable or threatened. Experiences like those lead to insights and breakthroughs. The combination of love and necessity has birthed a million social innovations. They didn't all spread far and wide. Many were invented to solve one problem. Yet those with wider potential have benefited from the interplay between disruptive, bridging and receptive innovators.

Wise travellers respect the roles and functions of each type of innovator. They know that social innovations not only emerge from relationships but also thrive and endure in relationships.

Becoming a Wise Traveller Means:
- Recognizing that the methods of the past aren't enough, by themselves, to tackle the challenges of the future
- Tapping into the passionate amateur in each of us
- Paying close attention to solutions developed by those who live at the literal and figurative margins of society; they awaken us to new possibilities
- Understanding that adversity turns into creativity when we love

HOW THE REGISTERED DISABILITY SAVINGS PLAN WORKS

The RDSP is a poverty-fighting tool for Canadians with disabilities. It can be set up at most financial institutions in the country. Anybody can contribute to the RDSP of a person with a disability. There is a lifetime contribution limit of $200,000, which can be made up of a few large payments or a series of small ones.

As a companion to the RDSP, the federal government offers the Canada Disability Savings Grant. The government will match RDSP contributions on a three-to-one, two-to-one or one-to-one basis, up to certain limits and depending on annual income.

A Canada Disability Savings Bond of up to $1,000 a year is also available to people with low income for twenty years.

The RDSP grows tax-free, and the assets do not disqualify people from receiving disability benefits. Funds taken from an RDSP cannot be clawed back by the disability benefit systems of most Canadian provinces and territories. There are few restrictions on what the funds can be spent on, and once a person becomes eligible, there are no reports to file.

EXAMPLE

If the parents of a baby born with a disability today contribute $1,500 a year to her RDSP for the next twenty years, the combination of matching grants, savings bond and compound interest will see her RDSP grow to about $250,000 by her thirtieth birthday. If she doesn't withdraw it all at once, her RDSP will become worth more than half a million dollars over her lifetime.

That's based on a total family contribution over twenty years of $30,000, or a little more than four dollars a day – the cost of a Tim Horton's double-double and a doughnut.

1

THINK AND ACT LIKE A MOVEMENT

···

*'cause it was in Bobcaygeon where I saw the constellations
reveal themselves one star at a time*

— The Tragically Hip, "Bobcaygeon"

In the late 1950s Marian Tompson began challenging doctors, hospitals and baby food giants about their role in fostering negative attitudes about breastfeeding. A self-described shy, stay-at-home mom in suburban Chicago, she and six other young mothers unintentionally launched a movement that introduced the "womanly art of breastfeeding" into the global lexicon. Marian co-founded La Leche League and served as its president for twenty-four years. Now La Leche has certified more than thirty thousand mother-to-mother leaders and three thousand groups in more than seventy countries.

During PLAN's early development, we were influenced by La Leche League and inspired by the group's success at remaining mother-led for so long. Many of PLAN's founding board members had started parent-run organizations focused on mutual support only to see them become professional-run and focused on service provision. We were determined to prevent that from happening. I was delighted when John McKnight, founder of the Asset-Based Community Development Institute, offered to introduce me to Marian in 2004.

In the late 1950s most moms in North America bottle-fed their infants. "About eighteen percent started out breastfeeding, but within a few weeks or months they stopped," Marian explained to me. "Nobody knew anything about breastfeeding in the hospital. Simple basic things. If I was worried about having enough milk, I didn't realize the more I nursed, the more milk I'd have. I didn't have any idea there was a connection. And neither did the doctors or hospital staff."

By the time I met Marian, she was described as the high priestess of breastfeeding, a mother of seven, grandmother of seventeen and great-grandmother of nine. She still had a determined sparkle in her eyes, and she was constantly working on new projects.

"I just thought it was so unfair that women who wanted the best for their babies couldn't get any help," she told me. This is as close as Marian gets to moral outrage. It's hard to believe she was branded a heretic by the medical establishment.

As word spread about the mothers' work, the phone calls and letters from moms asking for advice increased. Marian and the other women answered every letter by hand. To keep pace with the volume, they decided to collect their answers in a binder "held together with paper clips" and assembled on a kitchen table. As their expertise and confidence grew, they persuaded a publisher to produce a hardcover book, provided they could pay him a little at a time. They got an unexpected boost in 1963 when *Reader's Digest* profiled them in an article titled "They Teach the Joys of Breastfeeding." Within two months they'd sold ten thousand copies of their book, *The Womanly Art of Breastfeeding*.

La Leche never set out to create a movement. "We were helping our friends and people in the community," Marian recalled. "We just built it as the need arose. A lot came intuitively. We kept the jobs mother-sized, small enough so our families didn't suffer. We offered something no doctor could match – another mother at the end of the phone any time of the day and night."

Challenging medical authority was only one part of a broader cultural challenge. "We couldn't even use the word 'breast' in print when we started," Marian said. "Local papers said our meeting notices were unfit for family publications. That's why we decided on La Leche, which is Spanish for milk and the name of a shrine in St. Augustine, Florida, featuring a statue of the Christ child being breastfed. We had no idea it would spread and we would spend fifty years explaining what it meant!"

The twists and turns in La Leche's journey from those humble origins are spectacular. Now the world's foremost authority on breastfeeding, the League has through the years reached millions of mothers directly. It has reached even more indirectly, via the medical practitioners and institutions it has influenced.

Together, these women changed society's attitudes toward breastfeeding. When they began, very few mothers (less than ten percent) breastfed. Today the opposite is true.

Long May You Run

Marian Tompson and her companions didn't set out to create a movement.

You don't have to either. A movement is composed of a million small acts. It's impossible to predict which one will ignite a spark or cause the next surge. And it doesn't really matter.

What's most important is to recognize that you are already part of at least one movement. None of our passions, concerns or actions exist in a vacuum. Other people are confronting the same challenges, whether it's the health of our babies, poverty, violence or the degradation of the landscape. Movements help us pay attention to what else is going on. They connect the dots. They inform our actions. They encourage us to look up from our day-to-day individual and organizational priorities and link our efforts. If you unintentionally start a movement, so much the better.

Movements do two things better than other forms of organizing, such as committees, task forces, partnerships or coalitions.

First, movements provide a vehicle for collaborating and co-operating across sectors, organizational boundaries, social and economic strata, origins, backgrounds and jurisdictions. They are the ultimate inclusive container, encompassing the full assortment of actors required for transformative change.

Second, movements address the most critical yet elusive set of change variables: culture. I'm referring to those hard-to-change habits, beliefs, working relationships, authority flows and stories about the way things should be that most of us prefer to hang on to.

Movements change paradigms. They shift the boundaries of what is socially acceptable and expected. They provide a climate for new ideas. Institutional change cannot happen without movements. There are no shortcuts. Movements create favourable political conditions for legislative change, resource allocation and policy shifts to eventually occur.

Let me add one important caveat. Movements can be a force for good or for evil. Hitler came to power at the head of a mass movement. Other movements promote racism, sexism, fundamentalism, exclusion and genocide.

That's why it's important to anchor movement objectives to the values of social, financial and environmental justice. That's what the philosopher Charles Eisenstein meant when he encouraged the Occupy movement to focus on a world that works for everyone:

> This movement isn't about the 99% defeating or toppling the 1%. You know the next chapter of that story, which is that the 99% create a new 1%. That's not what it's about. What we want is to create the more beautiful world our hearts tell us is possible. A sacred world. A world that works for everybody. A world that is healing. A world of peace…. The system isn't working for the 1% either. If you were a CEO, you would be making the same choices they do…. Everybody wants to live a life of meaning.

Five Characteristics of Social Justice Movements

Although the word "movement" has become part of the vernacular, it's actually an enigmatic entity. As sociologist Troy Duster observed, "No movement is as coherent and integrated as it seems from afar, and no movement is as incoherent and fractured as it seems from up close."

Analyzing a movement's characteristics can help us figure out which elements we can influence, and perhaps strengthen and improve; which are beyond our expertise or reach; and which require more of our attention.

Progressive movements share the following five characteristics.

1. They Ignite Our Imaginations

I've learned a lot by studying the Abolition movement, which by my assessment is the first grassroots social justice movement ever. It started in 1787 when twelve abolitionists met in the back room of a London print shop, determined to abolish slavery. At the time, seventy-five percent of the world's people were either enslaved or in forced labour or serfdom. Slavery, not freedom, was the norm.

Those twelve individuals took on a task as daunting at the time as abolishing guns in the United States is today, as formidable as ending our current dependence on fossil fuel. Despite such humble beginnings, in the space of only twenty years they created enough momentum for the British Parliament to declare the slave trade illegal.

A contemporary of the abolitionists, Irish poet and songwriter Thomas Moore wrote: "It is my conviction that slight shifts in imagination have more impact on living than major efforts at change." Social movements strengthen our imaginative muscles. People gravitate to the possibility of movements and to the energy they attract and magnify. A bold, disruptive vision is a prerequisite for changing the status quo, its power structures, values and dominant beliefs. The vision provides the juice, converting outrage, passion and love into fuel for a long and tough journey.

2. They Are Multi-Generational

I once heard Aboriginal leader Georges Erasmus speak about the injustices experienced by First Nations, Inuit and Métis people in Canada. He was insistent that his people were not going away. "If you don't deal with my generation," I remember him saying, "our descendants are coming. If you don't deal with our sons and daughters, you'll have to deal with their children and their children's children."

Movements are destiny's children. Behaviour, habits and attitudes die slowly. The struggle is generational. The end of the slave trade in Britain in the early 1800s did not mean the end of slavery. It took another hundred years for the practice to be outlawed globally. And that was only the beginning. Racism is still a fact of life, and human trafficking is now a serious global issue.

Movements are the connective tissue for the identity and sense of belonging that characterize struggles for social justice. The question to ask isn't whether Idle No More, a movement started in 2012 to honour indigenous sovereignty, is over; it's where that aspect of the Aboriginal movement will surface again. What form will it take next? What will it merge with? No movement emerges in a vacuum. Idle no More has deep roots, and it honours the sacrifices of the ancestors.

3. They Comprise Small Acts

As John McKnight has observed, "If you have enough small stuff that's right, the big stuff will change." Seven determined mothers started La Leche League. They never imagined they would influence the World Health Organization's policy on breastfeeding. In 1971 a handful of Vancouver journalists and ecologists founded Greenpeace, and as a byproduct launched the modern environmental movement. Adelaide Hoodless's Women's Institute is credited with igniting the first wave of the women's movement, Betty Friedan's book *The Feminine Mystique* the next.

Movements are a collection of small acts. They emerge from a context in which thousands if not millions of individuals, networks and groups are feeling and acting on the same impulses. From their sparks, seemingly all of a sudden, a movement erupts.

History is not created by one man or one woman, Tolstoy believed, but by an infinitely large number of infinitesimally small actions. That's where you come in. Your small act – your book, organization, donation, protest, gathering, garden or YouTube video – might be the one that opens the floodgates.

4. They Are Self-Organizing

Brenda Zimmerman, a co-author of *Getting to Maybe*, describes movements as embodying order without central control. Movements operate less like machines and more like living systems – a school of fish, a flock of birds, the brain. Our brain has no central command structure. Different parts control our actions, thoughts and feelings at different times under different circumstances. Similarly, no one is ever really in charge of a movement. Leadership is diffuse.

The slow food movement, for example, started in 1986 as a reaction to fast-food restaurants in Italy, but it evolved into a fight against the standardization of food by the EU and the industrialization of food by agribusiness. Hidden amid the recipes in the cookbook *The Pleasures of Slow Food* is a compelling manifesto to protect centuries-old traditions of preparing and preserving food.

Today the slow food movement has grown to 100,000 members in 132 countries. And these groups exist shoulder to shoulder within a broader food movement that includes hundred-mile-diet proponents, seed-saving activists, organic farmers, anti-obesity campaigners, animal rights adherents, farmers' market organizers and permaculture experts.

Movements, to quote Leonard Cohen, "slide in all directions." They're not dependent on one driver, leader or champion. Who's leading? Who's following? It doesn't matter. It's more important to a movement's success that people complement one other's efforts, because that's what it takes to create a groundswell.

5. They Marry Art and Justice

Judith Marcuse, celebrated dancer and choreographer, believes that "Art bridges the silos that separate us as we confront today's pressing issues. Art creates new visions and engagement, connecting the head and the heart." Her belief led her to found the International Centre of Art for Social Change, a learning hub whose mandate links art with social innovation: "Art is central in helping people to find new ways to see the world and in developing models that integrate and celebrate imaginative thinking, leading to mobilization and effective action."

Budd Hall, founder of the University of Victoria's Office of Community-Based Research, has been tracking the evolution of movements into the twenty-first century. He suggests that movements are shifting from simply describing the world we want, to giving us the experience of what this new world would look like using the power of dance, drama, ritual, ceremony, poetry and humour. Movements, he says, are increasingly "about flow, networking, connectivity, immediacy, creativity and an immediate sensual intimacy."

The arts and social movements make a good marriage because they're both iconoclastic, set up by their very nature to challenge sacred cows. The arts elaborate culture. They lend movements compelling symbols and images that are more meaningful and hopeful than slogans and clichés. Royal Roads professor Catherine Etmanski suggests the arts are innately political in their "capacity to transform our perceptions of reality, and in the possibility that we will subsequently act upon those newly formed perceptions."

That quote nicely describes the work of Edward Burtynsky. His photographs and films of industrial landscapes expose the destructive impact humans are having on the earth. As he says about his exhibition *Water*, "My hope is that these pictures will stimulate a process of thinking about something essential to our survival; something we often take for granted – until it's gone."

PLAN's Fourfold Approach to Thinking and Acting like a Movement

I referred earlier to the disillusionment Vickie and I felt at PLAN's limited impact on the social isolation and poverty experienced by people with disabilities. A chance conversation with a close friend, Dr. Jan Christilaw, senior medical director of provincial women's health programs at BC Women's Hospital, helped me rethink our situation.

Jan was proud of the fact that BC Women's Hospital had been designated baby-friendly by both the World Health Organization and UNICEF. Today ninety-one percent of babies are being breastfed when they leave BC Women's. The hospital has stopped accepting free infant formula and baby bottles from manufacturers, plus it offers the only breast milk bank in Canada.

As I read the WHO citation, I was reminded of the work of La Leche League, although there was no acknowledgement of or reference to them. I began to see La Leche in a new light. In addition to their day-to-day support for new mothers, they coexisted with breastfeeding alliances, lactation consultants, certification programs, peer counselling training programs, baby-friendly hospitals and global institutions. The work of La Leche League was likely informing and inspiring those other groups, and vice versa. Collectively, they were creating impact.

This was a fork-in-the-road moment for me. I realized that one organization can't do everything and doesn't have to. Our expectations of PLAN, the organization, had been unrealistic.

When it was founded, PLAN too was already part of a movement – it was the parent arm of the disability movement. A key juncture in that movement came right after the Second World War. Groups of parents around the world rejected prevailing advice about their sons and daughters with intellectual disabilities and refused to send them to institutions. Instead, they set about creating the rich array of programs now available for people with disabilities and their families.

PLAN families were now thinking through the next phase. We didn't need to start a new movement, though perhaps we could offer a new burst of energy and insight to an existing one. Most importantly, we had to stop thinking we were on our own. We had to look up and see who else was around us.

An organization's job is to focus on its mission – to keep its hands in the soil. In PLAN's case its lifetime members had a very specific expectation: that PLAN would support their family member after the parents became infirm or died. That was a concrete organizational focus and a huge responsibility. Movements, on the other hand, give organizations a North Star, reminding them of the bigger picture and who else is heading in the same direction.

As the conversation evolved within PLAN, it became clear it wasn't about choosing one approach or the other. The board realized that unless we paid attention to the bigger picture, PLAN's work would always be marginalized. We needed an approach that would infuse our concepts and solutions into the broader disability ecosystem as well as into the wider culture. Vickie and I describe this as keeping one hand in the soil while stretching the other toward the stars.

As a result, in 2005 PLAN developed the following movement objectives:

- To embed a "full citizen" perspective in society's structures and institutions
- To shift the cultural consciousness of people with disabilities from needs and inability to contribution and participation

Vickie remembers her spine tingling when we first spoke those words out loud. They were bolder than anything we had ever imagined. We knew we couldn't achieve them on our own. We also knew we would never achieve them in our lifetime.

To even begin to close in on such ambitious objectives, PLAN needed a plan. Here is the fourfold methodology we developed for thinking and acting like a movement.

PLAN's Methodology for Thinking and Acting like a Movement

Doing: PLAN is still a learning laboratory. The important day-to-day work of supporting people with disabilities and their families continues, and those evolving experiences inform our broader agenda. Most important, our focus on the daily anchors our big-picture work, ensuring we don't get so far ahead of the parade that we can't hear the band.

Sharing: We created the PLAN Institute for Caring Citizenship to share our values, concepts and practices with other groups. We've established mentoring relationships with more than forty grassroots family groups around the world. We host annual retreats, publish books and manuals and offer online training. We've shared our work with interested groups such as family caregivers, people with chronic illness and seniors.

Changing: We realized PLAN's innovations would remain isolated unless they were embedded in public policy. For example, members of PLAN's personal networks had no legal status to represent or advocate on behalf of their friend or family member with a disability. This led to our involvement in establishing the Representation Agreement Act in British Columbia. This law legitimized caring, trusting relationships as a legal alternative to formal adult guardianship.

Inspiring: Innovators are not immune to reverting to the way they used to do things. It isn't easy to think yourself into a new way of acting. To address this inevitability, PLAN created ways for people to replenish their spirits, to be inspired, to engage in dialogue, to explore and to reflect. One important initiative was the Philia Dialogue on citizenship and disabilities. *Philia* is the Greek term for neighbourly love. As part of PLAN's movement objectives, we imagined an expanded definition of citizenship that welcomed everyone's contributions. We reached out to Canadian thought leaders and hosted dialogues with them throughout the country.

Each of these four sets of activities is essential for wider impact. Although they are interconnected, they move at different speeds. The work of doing happens daily. The turnaround time for sharing can be measured in months. Changing requires an investment of years. Inspiring may take decades to yield a harvest.

PLAN's fourfold methodology has allowed Vickie and me to work beyond the boundaries of the organization, while still staying anchored to PLAN's core values.

Conclusion

Wayne Gretzky wasn't the biggest hockey player in the NHL, or the fastest. Nor did he have the hardest shot. Yet he broke just about every scoring record in the league. His greatest asset has become mythical – he skated to where he intuited the puck would be. Once others caught on, they followed.

I've witnessed that same ability to anticipate and adjust at Ashoka, a global association of leading social entrepreneurs. Ashoka's leaders regularly review their role in the social enterprise movement by asking: Where is the social enterprise field headed?

Who do we need to partner with to get there? What are we doing that we no longer need to do, because others are doing it as well or better? How do we ensure our actions make a significant contribution to the field of social entrepreneurship?

All of us – individually, and through our coalitions, networks and organizations – are part of movements. We each play a role in the environment surrounding every challenge. Our daily decisions and behaviour can either support or undermine a movement's bold objectives. The value of movements lies less in reaching agreement on particular strategies or tactics than in getting as many vectors as possible moving in the same direction.

It's worth looking up regularly from our daily grind to see what else is going on, what we can learn from others and whether we are detracting from or enhancing a movement's objectives. By being intentional about our actions, we give greater lift to our collective aspirations.

Thinking and Acting Like a Movement Means:

- Acknowledging the movement(s) we are part of
- Choosing which parts of a movement's vision we are capable of implementing and which parts should be left to others
- Making our contribution, no matter how small or insignificant we think it is

SHARK TRUTH: COMBINING SOCIAL CHANGE AND CULTURAL HERITAGE

A great example of an organization thinking and acting like a movement is Shark Truth, a Vancouver group that aims to save sharks from extinction by preventing the consumption of shark fin products. Founder Claudia Li knew that in other cities that had enacted regulations to ban shark fin soup, the aftermath was often a community divided along racial lines. The regulations also left many ethnic Chinese feeling angry at environmentalists.

Li's approach is different. Not only does she want to promote shark conservation, she wants to enlist the largest ethnic minority in Canada as environmental activists.

Knowing that in her culture shark fin soup is a profound symbol of generosity, hospitality and celebration, Li began working with chefs to create tasty fin-free alternatives to shark fin soup, and with banquet caterers to promote fin-free weddings. To date the group she started has saved eight thousand sharks and stopped over eighty thousand bowls of shark fin from being consumed.

Just as important, by encouraging respect for a healthy ocean ecosystem, and by nurturing the values of sustainability and zero waste in the largest ethnic minority in Canada, Shark Truth is engaging more members of that community in environmental change.

Vickie and I met the former premier of British Columbia, Mike Harcourt, two years after he nearly died. In 2002 Mike had severely injured his spinal cord after falling from the oceanfront deck of his cabin. Thanks to his wife Becky's bravery and quick thinking, to the Pender Island Fire Department's rescue team and to his own fierce determination, Mike was back walking at about eighty percent capacity.

During Mike's recovery there had been a widespread outpouring of affection. Radio and TV host Vicki Gabereau described the entire province as holding its breath. Everyone wanted to shake his hand, including Vickie and me.

Our opportunity came because Mike was promoting social sustainability as chair of the Prime Minister's Advisory Committee for Cities and Communities. We were just starting our two-year exploration of social innovation and asked to meet him. We thought we'd be discussing the links between sustainability and social innovation. Instead, we got a lesson in "blue box-i-tizing."

If Mike had been a songwriter, he'd have worked at the Hit Factory. He has more hooks in his repertoire than most pop composers. His Harcourt-isms are populist and to the point. "Be discreet, don't use the streets," he advised while introducing an anti-solicitation bylaw. During BC's War in the Woods – a period of intense clashes between environmentalists, loggers, First Nations and government – he described himself as a "cool guy in a hot province." And he fondly describes the media as the "scrum of the earth."

In *Plan B: One Man's Journey from Tragedy to Triumph*, co-author John Lekich describes Mike as the "elder statesman of the Gore-Tex generation." He's gracious and likeable. I'd met him a few times, but he'd never quite got my name. He still calls me Al Atamanski, but I don't mind. I imagine he's really saying "Atta boy, Al." And that's the point. Mike is the kind of person who enters politics for the right reasons, stays decent and makes room for everyone.

2

CREATE A CONTAINER FOR YOUR CONTENT

The truth about stories is that that's all we are.
— Thomas King, The Truth about Stories

His office was small and unadorned, not the surroundings you'd expect for a senior politician who never lost an election, but fitting for a man in a hurry who left politics because, as he says, there's a sustainable world to organize. "Ten percent of any new initiative is the idea," he explained to Vickie and me. "The rest is implementation, and that's what I focus on. You have to be smart about cutting through inertia."

He continued with an example. "Count all the books written about the importance of recycling," he said. "All the reports and studies. All the ad campaigns. They hardly moved the dial at all. Then look what they did in Kitchener, Ontario, in 1983. They painted a plastic box blue, and today curbside recycling exists in hundreds of cities around the world."

His conclusion? "We have to blue box-i-tize our innovations, or they won't have widespread impact."

The Wisdom of Metaphor

Vancouver Island poet and philosopher Jan Zwicky believes that intelligent, musical use of language is important. She believes in the wisdom of metaphor:

> [W]hat a human mind must do in order to comprehend a metaphor is a version of what it must do in order to be wise. But of course we are not wise in a vacuum; we are wise about things, situations, people, the world. Thus,… those who think metaphorically are enabled to think truly because the shape of their thinking echoes the shape of the world.

Metaphors are much more than a literary device. They are essential to how we humans communicate, learn, discover and invent. A good metaphor alters the way we see things. It converts the complex to the vernacular. It creates an aha moment that insinuates itself into our consciousness.

Metaphors also influence our thoughts and behaviour. A University of Toronto study, for example, found that washing eases a guilty conscience. People who washed their hands after contemplating an unethical act were less troubled by their thoughts than those who didn't (although it didn't seem to work for Lady Macbeth and her "damned spot").

I think of metaphors as containers for content, as something into which you can put your ideas, statistics and proposals. Metaphors are essential for communicating beyond your base and for reaching people who aren't steeped in the issue and its accompanying jargon.

Content comes first, of course. You need to do your research and get the facts right. And your ideas have to be anchored by ethics. Above all else, as the Irish poet Seamus Heaney observed, we are "hunters and gatherers of values." If we lose touch with our values, we risk becoming spin doctors who gloss over tough realities or propagandists who manipulate people based on half-truths and half-baked assumptions.

However, literal or metaphorical containers offer an added benefit: their unconventionality helps your idea take hold. By offering a fresh perspective, they enliven an idea and make it accessible. They enable individuals to make sense of an idea from a personal point of view, thereby increasing their receptivity. Metaphors help people to withstand a barrage of facts and figures. And metaphors can breathe new life into an issue that has stalled because people are fatigued, overwhelmed or simply don't get it.

Presenting the right content in the right container makes it easier for people to do the right thing.

Five Characteristics of Effective Containers for Content

Thanks to Mike Harcourt, Vickie and I began seeing the equivalent of blue boxes everywhere. They were evidence of a creative process that went well beyond the hard work of analysis, invention and proof of concept.

Like Mike and Jan Zwicky, I like to think of containers as musical hooks that make ideas sing. Here are five characteristics of containers that resonate.

1. They Are Playful and Fun

Cycling along the back roads of my neighbourhood in South Surrey, particularly around Christmas, I notice that the deer images on road signs all have red noses. This is the good-humoured work of Operation Red Nose, a successful campaign to combat drinking and driving.

Every holiday season this national group invites people to "hand the reins over to us" and get home safe. One volunteer drives you home in your own vehicle after a night out, while another follows in a separate car to pick up the driver. Operation Red Nose understands that the reason you might risk driving after drinking is not the cost of a taxi but the hassle of picking up your car the next day.

Red Nose's founder, Jean-Marie De Koninck, one day heard a radio program about the number of accidents caused by impaired driving. A math professor and swim coach at Laval University, De Koninck was looking to raise funds for his swim team. By putting two and two together, he raised millions. Members of the swim team became the first drivers in a program that has since expanded to fifty-six thousand volunteers.

From a simple fundraising idea, De Koninck went on to develop a road safety campaign that benefits the population all year long. Since 1984 Operation Red Nose has partnered with police, insurance corporations, trial lawyer associations and financial institutions across Canada. Each year $1.5 million is distributed to more than a hundred nonprofit youth and amateur sports organizations.

In the courts of old, the royal jester was both an entertainer and a serious adviser to the monarch. Operation Red Nose is determined to reduce drinking and driving, but it has turned the admonition "don't drink and drive" on its head. By all means have

a good time and enjoy yourself, goes the message, just leave the
driving to us. As this example illustrates, it's possible for serious
work to be humorous and playful.

2. They Are Non-Judgmental

Ending violence against women and girls is a challenging goal to
achieve in Canada, as it is elsewhere in the world. Despite the
best efforts of women's shelters and other intervention programs,
the rates of relationship and family violence and sexual assault
remain high.

Sue Bookchin and Nancy Ross from Lunenburg County,
Nova Scotia, believed the situation wouldn't change as long as it
was seen as a women's issue, so they created Be the Peace to make
it a community issue. Their organization is reframing relationship
violence from a "bottomless pit" of pain and turmoil to what
they describe as a "'bottomless well' of wisdom, ingenuity and
commitment that resides in our community." The vision that guides
Be the Peace is for all women, girls, men and boys throughout
Lunenburg County to have satisfying relationships without
violence, or control over or disrespect for one another.

Be The Peace has decided to take blame out of the equation:

There is much judgment as we peer into situations of
domestic or relationship violence. From the outside
looking in, we make many assumptions about what is
going on, why it's going on, and what we think other
people should be doing. That is neither helpful nor inviting
if we wish to fully understand the root causes of violence
and how we can respond effectively both as individuals and
as a community.

Be the Peace calls its actions "peace plans." It aims for
truth but without blame or judgment, offering an alternative to the
perils of self-righteousness. The organization responds to the needs
of women and girls who have been abused, while acknowledging

that men and boys are also affected by violence and must be equal partners in ending it.

As is the case with all our tough challenges, it's important to recognize that blame has a limited shelf life. It gets people's backs up and weakens the potential for collaboration and constructive problem solving.

3. They Ignite Our Imaginations

For years the Kermode or spirit bear, a rare black bear with white fur, was a nuisance that plagued garbage dumps on the northwest coast of British Columbia. Then came the 1990s campaign to save Canada's Amazon, one of the largest remaining tracts of unspoiled temperate rainforest in the world.

The area stretches from the northern tip of Vancouver Island up to Alaska. Vickie and I have flown for hours over this ecological treasure, awed by its lush green forest, jagged fjords, blue-green lakes, tumbling waterfalls, glacier-covered mountain peaks and sheer pristine beauty, with few signs of human activity – no clear-cuts, forest roads, hydro lines or dwellings.

Maps matter-of-factly identified this area as the "Mid-coast and North-coast Timber Supply Areas." The campaigners, however, sought an image that would stir the imagination of consumers of forest products. They settled on the Great Bear Rainforest. The idea of protecting the Kermode bear and its habitat gave people a concrete way to understand what was at stake. As campaigner Darcy Riddell explained, "It also shifted the language being used about the region. It was no longer just a repository for wood, a valuable natural resource to be exploited; rather, it was a unique ecosystem and part of the natural heritage of the Earth."

This strategic reframing worked. In 2006 the Great Bear Rainforest Agreement was signed. It committed the BC government to protecting five million acres of rainforest and shifting forest management to a new ecosystem-based approach. In 2007 there followed a landmark conservation financing agreement, arranged by Tides Canada, that brought coastal First Nations communities

$120 million to support conservation management and economic development. To cap it off, BC adopted the spirit bear as one of the province's official emblems and made the Great Bear Rainforest an official region on its maps.

4. They Personalize the Abstract

The phrase "me to we" is an elegant example of the simplicity that lies on the other side of complexity. It personalizes the connection between wealth in North America and poverty in the developing world. It also shifts the focus from self-interest to collective responsibility. Me to We, now a movement with international reach, is the brainchild of the Keilburger brothers, Craig and Marc, who founded Free The Children when they were adolescents.

I met Marc when he became an Ashoka fellow in 2005. By then Free the Children had built 650 school and water projects in forty-five developing countries. But that wasn't good enough for a Harvard-trained Rhodes Scholar. "I realized no matter how many schools or sanitation projects we built, the underlying inequity originates in North America," he told me. He pointed out that this includes our lifestyle, consumption patterns and control of the world's economic distribution systems. "If we can change the awareness, attitudes and behaviour of the next generation in North America," he said, "we begin dealing with root causes."

Since then the brothers have expanded their focus. They founded Me to We in 2008. They published a book by the same name for young people and a corresponding curriculum for teachers. The organization now works with some of the biggest school districts in North America. Meanwhile, Free The Children has become the world's largest network of children helping children.

The brothers' family of organizations now includes annual We Days, which attract tens of thousands of young people to hear performances by stars like Justin Bieber, Kay, and Victoria Duffield, as well as high-calibre speakers like Jane Goodall and Olympic athlete Silken Laumann. Me to We has 2.3 million Facebook likes, making it the largest social media cause in Canada. It's also influencing traditional media, with Craig and Marc's weekly column running in newspapers across the country.

The many containers created by the Keilburgers are alerting millions of young people in the privileged world to their global responsibilities, and are shattering the stereotype of apathetic youth. Why is the brothers' work so successful? Because Craig and Marc have found ways of turning a huge, faraway issue into a cause that's real, that's up close and that you can do something about.

5. They Tell a Story

Each year Vickie and I lead a retreat based on the content of this book. No matter how hard we try for balance, we squeeze in too much. As a reprieve, at the end of every day we turn the program over to master storyteller David Roche.

It's a pivotal moment. Under David's guidance, people speak about what matters most to them. Nothing is canned or rehearsed. We get to know each other. We see beyond each other's titles, achievements and intellects. Many of our assumptions evaporate, and invariably, the energy shifts. We are no longer tired and the real learning begins.

It's an important reminder that we all want our side of the story to be heard. We all want to be part of a two-way conversation.

Stories get to the heart of the matter. Juno-nominated pianist and storyteller Michael Jones explains it this way:

> Too often our language is not large enough to articulate the vision we want to embrace. Story telling and story listening help us think and see in larger and more complex ways. They offer an integration that helps deepen the connection between the heart and mind. Together they create new neural pathways, connecting us with our own inner wisdom and helping us remember who we are, where we come from and what we most deeply want to be. Unlike

facts and data that identify the parts, stories carry the energy of the whole.

There is a rekindling of oral storytelling today, "with a variety of festivals, groups and gatherings giving storytellers new places to explore their art," according to Canadian storyteller Dan Yashinsky. "There is also a strong and growing interest in the way stories frame and flow through our everyday lives," he writes, "anchoring identity, preserving family heritage and building intercultural bridges."

Stories delivered via high-quality, well-distributed media are shifting social consciousness in a positive way. The TV show *Glee*, which features actor Lauren Potter, who has Down syndrome, as a cheerleader, has more successfully punctured disability myths than any public education spots I've been associated with. High-impact documentaries about pressing social issues, such as *The Cove* and the Academy Award–winning *Born Into Brothels*, are also reaching mass audiences.

Stories shift attitudes in a profound way. David Roche, who has a facial disfigurement, not only rescues the storyteller in each of us at our annual retreats, he also helps us conquer one of our deepest fears: our physical appearance. As he explains, "In its final form, a story is fundamentally a stirring in the hearts, minds and imagination of the audience."

Generating Your Own Media

Two days after its release in February 2013, more than a million people had seen *To This Day*, an animated anti-bullying video. The words are by Shane Koyczan, a spoken-word virtuoso who has been heard by more people around the world than any other Canadian poet. Inspired by teenager Amanda Todd, who committed suicide after being tormented online, the poem tells the story of Koyczan's own experience being bullied in school, as well as the narratives of two other victims, a girl with a birthmark on her face and a boy who suffers from depression.

Eighty-six artists and animators contributed to the video of *To This Day*. As of this writing, it's had more than twelve million views. The poem has an app, a website and a Wikipedia page and was published as a book by Annick Press. It also earned Koyczan an invitation to speak at TED Talks.

The video has been distributed by Upworthy, a group that approaches "social media with a mission: to make important stuff as viral as a video of some idiot surfing off his roof." They describe their audience as *The Daily Show* generation – people who care about what's going on in the world but don't want to be boring about it.

Nowadays groups like Upworthy, as well as blogs, Twitter feeds, Facebook, TED Talks, YouTube, Vimeo, podcasts, Netflix and video games, all compete with mainstream media for our attention. As Canadian journalist Beth Haddon said to a group of us, "The media environment has changed and journalism has been 'disrupted' by new technology more than any other modern industry." Haddon described a "new media cocktail composed of people formerly known as the audience." She believes that "non-journalists are now sources for news organizations, blurring the distinction between news and opinion and interactivity."

Social media, with its related devices, represents a revolution not only in communications but in collaboration. Networked media makes possible new forms of cooperation. The challenge is no longer finding an outlet for your message.

The new goal, according to Tracey Friesen, former executive producer at the National Film Board, is to create media that people pay attention to. Friesen observes that while many technical barriers to reaching mass audiences have been removed, the new space is crowded and noisy, and the material's effectiveness is often undermined by poor quality. Through an initiative called Story Money Impact, Friesen is working with activists, investors and directors to raise the standards for people-generated media. Her goal is to help filmmakers secure funds so that they can not only make movies with social impact, but also focus on audience development, outreach, social marketing, educational material and community tours.

PLAN's Search for the Right Container

PLAN had for two decades been demonstrating the value of personal networks, yet we could never get policy makers to take those networks seriously. We could show the emotional and spiritual benefits of our approach. We could prove that those in supportive relationships got sick less often and healed more quickly. We knew that people used fewer services when they had caring friends around them. Yet even this money-saving angle was politely ignored – until PLAN decided to launch Tyze Personal Networks.

Tyze is Vickie's brainchild, and she became its CEO. Through an online platform, Tyze organizes networks of support for people with disabilities, family caregivers, seniors and people with long-term illnesses such as cancer. Vickie jokes that Facebook is Tyze's major competitor, but the fact is, you can't search the web for a Tyze network. Each network is private, and there is no advertising or data mining. Tyze networks are personal, not social. Tyze friends are real, and their number is limited to people you can count on.

The success of Tyze is merely a step along the way. Vickie wants to spread the benefits of a network model of care to millions. Her bolder ambition is to spark a policy shift – to see policy move from an individual focus toward a network-centric model of care. Until she developed the Tyze container, that ambition was an elusive dream. Thanks to Tyze, it's becoming a reality.

Tyze has spread rapidly in Canada, the US and the UK, with ten thousand users to date. After just a few years, it is already benefiting substantially more people than did PLAN's previous two decades of network development.

Equally important, Tyze has attracted the attention of governments. Vickie has worked with the Prime Minister's Office in Canada, the British Cabinet Office and various government ministries and departments in Canada and the US. Major funders like the McConnell Family Foundation in Canada and the Robert Wood Johnson Foundation in the US have invested in Tyze's spread. Major service providers, such as Saint Elizabeth Health Care, the largest home care provider in Canada, are offering it to their clients. In fact, so attracted was Saint Elizabeth to Tyze that they recently bought the company and are expanding its reach.

Creating the Tyze container was critical for spreading PLAN's approach to care beyond people with disabilities. The advent of web-based networks made it easier for people to understand and support a network model of care.

Conclusion

"The medium is the message" is one of the most famous sayings coined by a Canadian. Marshall McLuhan was referring to the symbiotic relationship between content and container. He was also suggesting that the container's characteristics affect culture as much as the content does, since containers are metaphors through which we conceptualize reality.

When we find the perfect match between content and container, we build bridges between poetics and politics and between image and imagination. In Beth Haddon's words, we "widen the tent, reach out to the larger society and offer people new and better ways of doing things."

Creating a Container for Your Content Means:
- Using metaphor to make it easy for people to do the right thing
- Telling your story
- Breathing life into issues that affect us all

THE FOUR PILLARS APPROACH

For intravenous drug users in the late 1990s, Vancouver's Downtown Eastside was closer to hell than paradise. There was a reason the area was known as the Killing Fields. Vancouver had the highest drug overdose death rate in Canada – nearly 200 people in 1998 alone – and HIV rates were the highest in the western world.

Into this void stepped Donald MacPherson from the City of Vancouver's Carnegie Community Centre. Donald introduced Vancouver to the revolutionary policy of harm reduction by finding the right container, the four pillars approach, in which to present it.

Medical professionals, community activists and drug users themselves knew that neither arresting users nor trying to stop the flow of illicit drugs into the area was working. The harder drugs were to get, the greater their worth in the marketplace and the more crimes people committed to pay for their habit. The result was climbing rates of HIV infection and death and increasing police costs.

Nevertheless, official policy and cultural beliefs about prohibition were intertwined and ingrained. "We'll rehabilitate you only when you stop using," the thinking went. "Whatever happens to you in the meantime is your responsibility, not ours." As Diane Riley, a founding member of the International Harm Reduction Association, put it, "This war [on drugs] is more akin to a Crusade, in which there can be no victory but only some distorted sense of moral superiority."

Donald MacPherson, who had taken a leave of absence from work to visit Zurich (an intuitive decision, he told me – see Pattern Six), knew that the Swiss had pioneered a way to reduce death, infection and policing costs related to IV drug use. Their method also provided humane treatment for users and increased their chances of rehabilitation. A key component was safe injection sites, an approach Donald knew would work in Vancouver. Yet no political leader in the city could afford to be seen sanctioning drug use. The mayor at the time, Philip

Owen, declared that he was totally and violently opposed to the move. Instead, he believed in twenty-five-year mandatory life sentences.

On the other hand, there was political consensus in the city about three approaches: prevention, treatment and enforcement. So that's where Donald started. First he proposed the so-called four pillars drug strategy, with harm reduction as the fourth pillar. Then he defined harm reduction to include reducing harm to the community as well as the drug-dependent individual. Finally, he embedded a safe injection site into the harm reduction strategy.

The swerve worked. Although there were bumps along the road, agreement was surprisingly quick. Each pillar was seen as indispensable, and all were interconnected.

The overall psychological effect of the four pillars approach was significant. It conveyed a sense that civic leaders knew what they were doing. It gave the public an easy way to digest a complex situation. And it overcame Vancouverites' sense of helplessness: they could better understand the choices involved and could play a role in stopping the spiral.

Mayor Owen went on to become the first political champion of harm reduction in Canada. Every Vancouver mayor and British Columbia premier since 2001 has endorsed the four pillars drug strategy and its most controversial component, Insite, a supervised injection site. So have subsequent police chiefs and medical health officers. It has become part of Vancouver's culture.

Deaths have plummeted. More than thirty peer-reviewed studies have shown that Insite saves both lives and health care dollars, reduces the spread of disease and promotes entry into addiction treatment. The site survives despite the federal government's attempts to shut it down. Sadly, Insite remains the only government-approved safe injection site in North America.

After leaving the City of Vancouver in 2009, Donald MacPherson helped form the Canadian Drug Policy Coalition to promote harm reduction throughout Canada. He is also working with Adam Kahane and the Organization of American States on what Juan Manuel Santos, president of Colombia, calls a global rethink on the war on drugs. The OAS report will be presented at a special meeting of the United Nations General Assembly in 2016.

3

SET THE TABLE FOR ALLIES, ADVERSARIES AND STRANGERS

...connections are the harness that pulls your wagon.
— Guy Vanderhaeghe, *A Good Man*

Civility is Paul Born's operating system. Since Born is based in Waterloo, Ontario, the birthplace of the BlackBerry, I couldn't resist the analogy.

Other similarities connect Paul and the BlackBerry's co-founders. Mike Lazaridis and Jim Balsillie used their talent to make phones smarter. Paul uses his to make cities smarter about reducing poverty. Research in Motion was once the dominant telecommunications company in the world. Paul's organization, Vibrant Communities, is the dominant anti-poverty collaboration in Canada, perhaps North America. And US President Barack Obama is a big fan of both technologies. Besides being a die-hard Blackberry user, Obama has made Paul's book *Community Conversations* mandatory reading for the White House Council for Community Solutions.

I would often run into Paul as we criss-crossed the country. We got along well, usually heading out for long walks in whatever city we happened to be in. Paul has the size and personality of an opera tenor. The word "gusto" best describes his embrace of conversations, especially the kind he calls "big, messy and purposeful." It was on one of our walks that I discovered Paul's spirit is as huge as his talent.

Paul started as a traditional community organizer. Identify the problem, target a solution, organize, problem solved – or so the thinking went. He spent twelve years building the Community Opportunities Development Association in the Kitchener-Waterloo area. CODA helped five and a half thousand people get back to work and twelve hundred unemployed people start small businesses. The United Nations awarded CODA for developing one of the forty best poverty-fighting practices in the world.

Yet Paul was stymied. No matter how many people CODA helped, overall poverty in Kitchener-Waterloo kept rising. At the UN reception, Paul actually stood up and said, "With all due respect, instead of giving me this award you should be firing me." Something had to change.

On one late-night walk around Montreal's Mount Royal, Paul described his conversion from community organizer to convener. First he handed another agency the important task of helping people find jobs. Then he and his colleagues decided to get the whole Kitchener-Waterloo community talking about poverty. "An employment program only deals with one aspect of a complex challenge like poverty," he explained. "You need a united front to respond to the overall economic and social health of neighbourhoods as well as to combat related problems like racism or indifference."

Dialogue can seem like a circuitous route, but it eventually led to the Waterloo region claiming the lowest poverty rate in the country. Paul wrote about it this way: "We reached this milestone as a community by talking together across sectors, working together without judgment, and thinking differently about how to help those in need." That was the genesis of his new organization, Vibrant Communities.

According to Paul, powerful conversations are like a tide that lifts all boats. They enable real and lasting change. Thanks to Vibrant Communities, more than one hundred Canadian cities now have poverty-fighting roundtables. Those roundtables in turn have encouraged nine provinces to adopt anti-poverty strategies. Paul is confident that the remaining province will soon get on board.

Modern communication technologies come and go. But old-fashioned conversation remains vibrant, the true nature of its power waiting to be rediscovered.

The Power of Conversational Space

What I've identified as the third pattern in this book is the one that most surprised me.

Convening and dialogue are not just the means to an end; they are important ends in themselves. Before meeting Paul, I'd seen conversation as a mere tool – important, but just part of the process. After all, campaigners have been bringing people together forever. But today's conveners have diagnosed a breakdown of trust, both within civil society and between civil society, government and business. Unless that trust is restored, achieving social, economic and ecological justice will be impossible.

According to Canadian philosopher Mark Kingwell, justice is dialogic, not static. He suggests that our focus must shift from legal norms and statutes into the conversational spaces where justice is generated and renewed. This shift highlights the importance of the talkers who do the generating and renewing. Dialogue gives us the opportunity to meet one of our deepest needs, the need to belong. It's a vehicle for becoming part of something larger than ourselves, which to Kingwell is what citizenship is all about. "Citizenship is a way of making concrete the ethical commitments of care and respect, of realizing in action an obligation to aid fellow travelers – in short, of fostering justice between persons." Out of the incubational space of dialogue, citizens are reborn.

There is no contradiction between dialogue and action. Today's conveners take the time to set the table properly for all the people who can contribute to the success of the initiative being promoted. They know that the right setting can foster an appreciation for everyone's authenticity and caring. It can steer dialogue closer to a shared vision of the future. It can help those around the table agree on the challenges and commit to looking for solutions together.

The Challenge of Working Together

Breaking up may be hard to do, but working together is even harder. That was certainly evident in the early days of Social Innovation Generation, or SiG.

After Vickie and I finished our two-year exploration of social innovation in 2006, the McConnell Foundation decided to keep the ball rolling by establishing SiG. The partnership included the foundation itself as well as the PLAN Institute, Toronto's MaRS Discovery District and Waterloo's Institute for Social Innovation and Resilience. I became one of the partners, while Vickie returned to her work at PLAN.

SiG's mandate was to inspire a culture of social innovation, to bring out the best of Canadian ingenuity. Surprisingly, we brought out the worst in each other. Our early meetings were unpleasant and tense. We were often rude and offensive. We blamed each other and pursued arguments beyond their expiry date. I pouted and silently fumed during many of our gatherings, swearing I'd never go back. In fact, I quit twice.

We're still sorting out the reasons for the rocky start. Poet Elizabeth Smart referred to the "stadium of her ego." Egos certainly competed for space at the SiG table. So did our titles, status and authority. The biggest factor, however, was our discomfort with ambiguity and uncertainty. We had no idea what a culture of social innovation would look like, let alone how to get there. Our insecurities exposed, each of us tried to fight uncertainty with certainty – the certainty of our intellectual beliefs, our biases about how change should be made, our job titles and the faults of the other SiG partners, which we could see more clearly than our own.

This was not the kind of behaviour you'd expect from people who liked and respected each other (and still do, by the way). But it did reflect the messiness of working together when you're giving birth to something new, something different. It takes time for our behaviour to catch up with our aspirations. Insecurity is a natural manifestation of heading into the unknown.

It took us two years at SiG to deal with our confusion, doubt and conflict, a period when it wasn't certain that success was possible or that the initiative would continue. In effect, we had to shift our own culture before we could foster a culture of social innovation in others.

Because we couldn't handle the intensity of our interactions, we hired a national coordinator. This liberated each of the four partners to pursue goals compatible with our expertise and interests, knowing that someone else would coordinate our efforts. That took the pressure off, but we lost our creative spark. I still wonder whether the unintended consequence was a stifling of deeper insights about working together on deeply rooted problems. I am still feasting on this experience and expect to do so for years. It touched every fragile nerve of mine.

Our experience at SiG illustrates how difficult it is to work with friends and allies, let alone people who have hurt or betrayed us, or those who oppose us, or those we don't know.

Let's be honest: like anyone else, community activists can at times be territorial, competitive and suspicious of each other. We ignore what others are doing. We deal with conflict by forming another group. Heaven forbid we should try to work out our differences.

Yet we've arrived at a time in history when we can no longer afford to work in parallel, let alone at loggerheads. Although there's lots of rhetoric about working together, the challenges are tougher than we think. And we need to overcome them.

Four Characteristics of Effective Convening

How we set the table matters. It's important to get this right. Our convening has to be better than just good enough. It's not as simple as "schedule a meeting and they will come." We've all been part of processes that have led nowhere, that have let the air out of the room. As a result, we're often hesitant about talkfests.

Fortunately, we've learned a lot about working together effectively in the last fifty years. I'm thinking of approaches like appreciative inquiry, integral theory, future search, scenario planning, chaordic design, social innovation labs, the Art of

Hosting, Enterprise Facilitation, World Café, Open Space and Theory U.

These and other processes and methodologies have emerged as thoughtful disciplines to "revolutionize how we work together," as Kate Sutherland puts it in her useful book *Make Light Work in Groups*. The most effective of the processes rest on four principles.

1. Civility

I recall participating in one dialogue that got out of control. The head of an economic think tank was dispensing advice to a fellow participant, a single mother. "If you care about your children," he said, "you should leave your neighbourhood. Staying and trying to make your neighbourhood better is self-indulgent. I wouldn't raise my children there. Neither should you." His arrogance and ignorance were dreadful. My polite silence was worse.

Civility goes deeper than being polite or courteous. Politeness can simply be a way of avoiding the tough conversations, of not expressing your views for fear of offending. There must be an ethic of substance behind our manners. Getting to the root of issues requires lively and tough conversations.

Civility is a social lubricant for resolving conflict, for handling dissent and for working together. It offers guidelines not only for when to voice our opinions but for how to voice them. Civility encourages us to:
- criticize with kindness: for example, to acknowledge points of agreement and anything you may have learned from your opponent
- represent a position without being offensive
- be simultaneously forceful and respectful
- respect the other without necessarily liking them
- move beyond political correctness and moral righteousness
- avoid caricature

Mark Kingwell offers an intriguing metaphor. He reminds us that stones are polished by tumbling together, by the friction of interacting. Civility provides us with the opportunity to polish each other, he writes, "not only so that rough spots and edges may be removed, but also so that one may begin to reflect another in the common social project of public life."

2. Personal Agency

Skilled community organizers understand that people will be committed to act on what they've had a hand in creating. That's why Paul Born starts every gathering he leads by asking: Why is it important that you are here? "You become a doer as soon as you answer that," Paul says. "It connects the heart and the brain."

Conveners strive to bring out the best in everyone. They convene around gifts. They cheer people on, shining a light on their accomplishments and on what they could achieve together. If conveners usually enter a room composed of leaders and followers, they hope to leave a room full of leaders, people who are emboldened and willing to take responsibility for what they say and do. Front-of-the-room leadership isn't enough. Neither is leadership that suggests they will do it all for you.

As Ashoka founder and CEO Bill Drayton puts it:

> The most important contribution any of us can make now is not to solve any particular problem, no matter how urgent energy or environment or financial regulation is. What we must do now is increase the proportion of humans who know that they can cause change.

3. Hospitality

I once watched in fascination as John Ralston Saul, one of the world's most popular speakers, got down on his knees to measure the space between chairs. This happened a few hours before a dialogue John and I were hosting began. John was paying as much attention in advance to the look and feel of the room – the aesthetics, the colour, the food and the participants' legroom – as he would later to his remarks.

John wants people to feel welcome and comfortable, and he knows the secret is in the details. Conveners set their tables as thoughtfully as a chef preparing a great feast. They do their best to make over the physical space in which people will gather, including dreaded hotel meeting rooms. They seek, according to Peter Block, author of *Community: The Structure of Belonging*, to "bring the room into life and life into the room."

Conveners are reviving the ancient art of hospitality. They want to transform isolation and self-interest among the people they set places for, who are often strangers to each other, into connection and belonging. Their intent is to reflect, as much as possible, the world around them. They want people from diverse perspectives – people who will be affected by the outcome as well as people with the authority to make decisions. Everyone counts, and positions based on power, authority and resources must not dominate. Effective conveners employ an abundance mindset and are able to explain why each participant's contribution is essential.

Hospitable design creates the conditions for new kinds of conversations to occur, for new approaches to emerge, for the unpredictable to happen and for everyone to succeed. To quote Peter Block again, conveners strive to create a sense of belonging, "to transform the isolation and self-interest within our communities into connectedness and caring for the whole."

4. Curiosity

Alice Munro's short stories revolve around the theme that life is full of surprises. Her stories don't suggest that everything will turn out well, just that things will turn out in ways we can't foresee. She reminds us that life is serendipitous and that only the unexpected is predictable.

An important condition of convening is curiosity – about the other, about the challenge, about ourselves and about deeper patterns. Conveners bring out our curiosity, not our certainty. They remind us we are on a journey of discovery into uncharted territory. They "hold the space" for something new to emerge. After all, if we knew the solution, we'd need a strategic plan, not a dialogue.

Paul Born explains the importance of curiosity like this:

> It's not about changing anything. For example, the poverty system is already changing. It's about welcoming you to participate in that which is already changing. Change has been brewing for a long time. We're all newcomers, and the best thing we can do is listen. Listen with respect to what the problem is telling us. Try to spot the patterns that are keeping the particular system unhealthy and help it heal itself.

Conveners have the confidence and the discipline to wait for insight. They are comfortable with mystery and have faith that something relevant will emerge. They soften our impatience and they soothe our fears – of failure and of being criticized for not doing something. They invite us to pay attention to the challenges, contradictions and paradoxes a system is trying to resolve.

New Approaches to Convening

There are various new ways of working together that embody the methods and principles I've outlined above. Three of the most promising are crowdsourcing, web-based collaborations and social innovation labs.

Crowdsourcing

Ashoka Changemakers uses web competitions to invite solutions to social and environmental challenges from the widest possible audience. According to Delyse Sylvester, who has coordinated sixty of these competitions, one that had a huge impact was the SME Finance Challenge, the first ever competition launched by the G20.

Small and medium enterprises, or SMEs, account for most of the world's job creation. They pull people out of poverty and contribute to the economic stability of developing economies.

Sylvester, who is based in Nelson, British Columbia, worked with Canada's then finance minister, Jim Flaherty, who invested $20 million. By the time the final entries were announced at the G20 Seoul Summit in 2010, the SME Finance Challenge had leveraged another $0.5 billion.

One of the winning entries was the Ottawa-based Peace Dividend Trust, since renamed Building Markets. This group encourages international donors (governments and charities) to contract with local suppliers in developing countries to provide labour and materials for projects like building schools and roads, rather than bringing in resources from outside. The idea is to boost the economic and strategic impact of peace and humanitarian missions by building local markets and creating local jobs.

Building Markets helps local enterprises win these procurement contracts by giving them lines of credit and connecting them to domestic, regional and global supply chains. Currently working in Haiti, Liberia, Timor-Leste, Myanmar and Afghanistan, Building Markets has redirected more than $2 billion to local economies and created sixty-five thousand jobs.

Delyse Sylvester knows that crowdsourced solutions attract fresh thinking and harness it quickly. They shorten the time it takes to get a good idea in front of funders and investors. This in turn reduces transaction costs. Crowdsourcing attracts input not just from mainstream groups but also from disruptive innovators who might not have the resources or know-how to get their ideas to traditional funders. As they did with the SME Finance Challenge, crowdsourced solutions can stitch together a global online community of social innovators, creating a platform for future collaboration.

Web-Based Collaborations

A new breed of activists are using web-based tools to achieve social change. They see in the hidden architecture of the web a democratic structure with the potential to engage more people in thoughtful, informed decision-making.

A charter member of that group is Jason Mogus. Founder and CEO of Communicopia, he is one of the world's foremost digital strategists. He has won a Webby (the web equivalent of an Oscar) and a We Media Game Changer award for his work. In 2001 he founded the Web of Change series of conferences to connect people and organizations that work at the intersection of technology and social change.

Mogus has been in the digital trenches since the web's infancy. He sees behind and beyond the dazzle of technology and social media, understanding that they're not substitutes but rather supplements for the tough, messy work of campaigning and movement building. He does, however, believe the web can precipitate and accelerate this work if network thinking is built into the design. This network effect, he says, will "lower the friction involved with sharing, and pour gas on small fires that catch."

Communicopia's clients include Tar Sands Solutions Network, Human Rights Watch, The Elders, Nothing But Nets and TckTckTck. This last was the first attempt to convene a global alliance of the world's largest environmental NGOs and international development NGOs that focus on climate change. TckTckTck asked Mogus, during the UN Climate Summit in Copenhagen, to design a digital campaign to coordinate the main players' actions, broaden the base of supporters and align the key messages.

While the Copenhagen Accord didn't produce the hoped-for commitments from government leaders to deal with climate change, it did make the public more aware of the need to take action. It also proved that an assortment of more than two hundred civil society organizations could work together, despite not knowing each other, despite having different mandates, despite egos and geography.

That collaboration continues. So does the engagement of seventeen million global citizens for climate action, who will light many fires. Jason Mogus is buoyed by the prospects of mobilizing a global movement around climate change. As he says, "Movements are bigger than brands."

Social Innovation Labs

Social innovation labs bring together people from diverse perspectives to explore, experiment, create prototypes and carry out solutions to hard-to-solve problems. These labs are stealing a page from business, technology, medicine and science, fields where R&D and experimentation are not only acceptable but necessary to retain market share, improve products and services, and discover breakthroughs. For example, it took James Dyson, one of the UK's most famous contemporary inventors, 5,127 prototypes to develop the world's first cyclonic bagless vacuum cleaner – meaning 5,126 of the prototypes were failures. "But," Dyson has said, "each failure was necessary for me to improve and perfect my technology."

Social innovation labs provide a safe place to experiment, learn, innovate and even fail without harming potential beneficiaries. They're organized around many topics, from aging to homelessness to sustainable food.

Some labs are social enterprises, like the Netherlands' Kennisland (Knowledgeland), whose mission is to make society smarter in the belief that "a smart society is one that works together." Some are government-owned, like the Danish MindLab, a self-described "cross-governmental innovation unit which involves citizens and businesses in creating new solutions for society." Others are hosted at universities, like MIT's Media Lab, which concentrates on "design and technologies that address social causes." Still others bring together communities of interest, like the UK-based Finance Innovation Lab, which is "incubating and accelerating new forms of prosperity. For people and planet."

Labs are popping up in Canada too. Witness Montreal's Institut du Nouveau Monde, which launched LABIS, "a collaborative process for finding solutions to complex social problems." Or George Brown College's Institute Without Boundaries, a Toronto-based studio "that works towards collaborative design action and seeks to achieve social, ecological and economic innovation." Or CityStudio, an innovation hub within Vancouver City Hall that gathers staff, university students and the community to work on sustainable solutions. Or The Natural Step Canada, whose Sustainability Transition Lab addresses barriers to sustainability. Or the MaRS Solutions Lab, which offers "a dedicated space to explore and trial new solutions that help sticky problems get unstuck."

Regardless of their purpose or origin, social innovation labs do many things:

- help people from different sectors, perspectives and backgrounds to develop a common understanding of "the problem," including those affected by the problem and those with the power or resources to do something about it
- allow the interconnections and complexities of an issue to be explored
- enable participants to experiment, test and work out the kinks to proposed solutions in a disciplined environment
- foster solutions based on the experiences and perspectives of the user or beneficiary
- lead to implementation strategies that address the structural and cultural aspects of change

The Philia Dialogue

Around the same time Paul Born was recognizing the limits of program-based solutions to reducing poverty, Vickie and I were realizing that while you can pass laws against discrimination and enact human rights legislation, you can't legislate against low expectations. Too often the general public focuses on the diagnosis and the label that a person with a disability has been given. They assume incapacity. They assume the individual has no gift or contribution to make. These conclusions breed a vicious spiral of faulty assumptions that can become a self-fulfilling prophecy.

We decided to tackle this challenge of prevailing cultural attitudes head on. In 2005, together with community leaders and organizations inside and outside the disability field, PLAN created the Philia Dialogue. Philia's mandate was to explore the concept of caring citizenship from the perspective of people with disabilities. Philia asserted that everyone, regardless of label, condition, diagnosis or age, not only has a contribution to make but must be expected to make it. The health, well-being and strength of society require the presence and participation of everyone.

For the next five years, thanks to funding from the McConnell Foundation, Philia convened conversations across Canada around the notion of caring citizenship. We explored such foundational values as civility, compassion, justice, courage, reciprocity, trust, forgiveness and hospitality. Our most effective approach was to partner with remarkable Canadian thought leaders, including Bonnie Sherr Klein, John Ralston Saul, Catherine Frazee, Michael Ignatieff and Mark Kingwell. We reasoned that these people already had an audience, which guaranteed us one too.

Together we developed an inclusive definition of citizenship. Our thought leaders published articles on the subject and referred to Philia in books they were writing. Mark changed his philosophy curriculum at the University of Toronto. John became PLAN's patron. Michael included a reference to Philia in one of his Massey Lectures. Bonnie and Catherine made the film *Shameless: The Art of Disability*.

As a testament to the surprising path our dialogues took, I was once in a New York bookstore looking at a new book on citizenship when a passage caught my eye. Thinking it would be a good resource for the Philia website, I checked the footnote only to discover the author was referencing Philia.

Today disability policy at the federal and provincial levels is citizen-focused, and there's now a Centre for Inclusion and Citizenship at the University of British Columbia. We'd like

to think the Philia Dialogues had something to do with these
developments.

Conclusion

The expression "At least they're still talking" resonates for most
Canadians. In the middle of the last century, our country had
a reputation for peacemaking, which culminated in the Nobel
Peace Prize being awarded to Lester Pearson. Andrew Cohen, in
his biography of the former prime minister, described Pearson's
role in resolving the Suez crisis as that of midwife. To Pearson, as
to all good conveners, process mattered. Cohen notes the human
elements of his diplomacy: "Patience, empathy, and the ability to
understand another's reality."

Fortunately, the Canadian aptitude for peacemaking
and diplomacy hasn't disappeared. It's being applied to a variety
of domestic challenges, as the people and initiatives described in
Pattern Three reveal. These domestic peacemakers know they're
not starting from scratch. They believe in the human capacity to
put aside differences. They provide opportunities for trust between
people to grow. They give birth to understanding.

Setting the Table for Allies, Adversaries and Strangers Means:
- Working together with those we don't like, don't trust or don't
  know, despite our differences or past wrongs
- Recognizing that thinking, reflecting, listening and talking are
  as essential as action
- Being open to surprise and serendipity
- Rising again and rising above

BC SOCIAL INNOVATION COUNCIL: PERFECTLY ORDERED DISORDER

. . . [S]ocial innovation profoundly impacts an existing challenge while increasing our resources to tackle the inevitable next set of challenges.

– From *Together: Respecting Our Future*, BC Advisory Council on Social Innovation

I turned down the former premier of British Columbia, Gordon Campbell, when he asked me in 2010 to chair the BC Council on Social Innovation. Well, sort of.

Actually, Gord Hogg and I had a slightly better idea. Gord had just been appointed BC's first parliamentary secretary for social innovation (and the first in Canada). Gord and I wanted to do more than produce a report that would gather dust. We were both old enough to have seen faulty assumptions, misunderstandings and past grievances derail the implementation of even the best recommendations. Further, we knew the recommendations from such a council would just scratch the surface. We needed something that would last longer than the Social Innovation Council's tenure, produce recommendations that would be acted on and set the stage for future ideas.

I accepted Gordon Campbell's invitation but recommended that a representative from business and another from government join me as co-chairs. Gord Hogg made a few other tweaks as well. He proposed a structure that would maximize the chances for people to get to know each other within and across sectors. This included:

- creating an assistant deputy minister's committee on social innovation to implement the recommendations, the chair of which would also be the government co-chair of the Social Innovation Council
- having both the ADM committee and the Council report to Gord Hogg as parliamentary secretary for social innovation (typically, public servants don't report directly to a politician other than their minister)

- inviting the official Opposition to send a representative to Council meetings (typically, elected Opposition members aren't invited to sit on government-appointed committees)

This combination of multi-sector co-chairs, this blend of elected officials and public servants, and this spirit of non-partisanship had never been tried before in BC. Someone suggested that it fit the words of Canadian painter and writer Emily Carr: "Perfectly ordered disorder designed with a helter-skelter magnificence." From the outside it seemed unruly, but it worked.

In 2012 the Council produced eleven recommendations, one of which was to establish BC Partners for Social Impact as an independent successor to the Council. The new group's mandate is to:

- work with the BC government to make sure the Council's recommendations are implemented
- make connections and promote engagement among social innovators, social entrepreneurs, academics, business and government in the province
- identify emerging barriers to social innovation in BC

Partners for Social Impact has the same co-chair arrangement the Council did, with direct links to the internal ADM committee and politicians. One big difference is that in 2013 BC Premier Christy Clark appointed a minister for social innovation — a first, we are told, in the world.

One hopeful sign is that a new story about social change is emerging in BC. Observes David LePage, a leading social entrepreneur, "Before, BC was content to be known as a province that produced pioneering social entrepreneurs. Now we are proud to be a province that is learning to work together to solve our social problems."

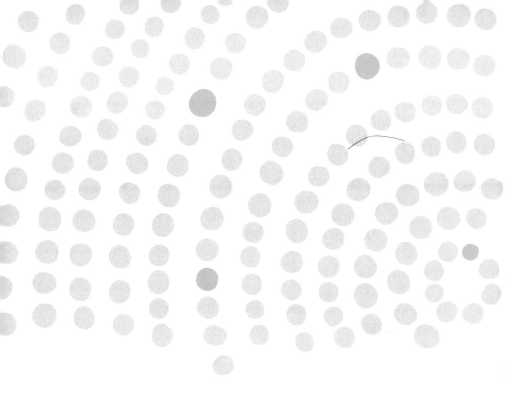

4

MOBILIZE YOUR ECONOMIC POWER

In a democracy people don't sit in the social and economic bleachers; they all play the game.

— Rev. Dr. Moses Coady

We slumped into the seats of the first coffee shop we could find. "My brain hurts," said Vickie. "Mine's bursting too," I replied. "I'm not sure how much of that I retained." After a long day at Ashoka's global headquarters in Arlington, Virginia, we were beat. Our brains felt enlarged, throbbing with new blood. Our weariness had a strangely delicious quality.

Ashoka is a global organization that identifies and invests in social entrepreneurs and helps them make an impact. Ever since I'd been appointed as a fellow, in 2003, visits to Ashoka had become an indispensable part of our social innovation exploration.

Vickie and I had spent the afternoon with Bill Kelly, a long-time Ashoka board member. Tall, courtly and gracious, Bill embodies Ashoka at its most hospitable. He and his wife, Cindy, hosted us during our frequent visits, putting us up in their guest room. Their dinners introduced us to some of the most inspiring people we'd ever met. I got to know Bill better during our early-morning bicycle rides through the parks and along the rail trails and canal towpaths of their Washington, DC, neighbourhood. He usually set up the schedule when Vickie and I visited. There wasn't a resource or contact he couldn't and wouldn't find for us. Ashoka is like that: nurturing and supportive.

On this particular day Bill had asked to meet us for a late lunch. He must have thought we were ready, because as we ate, he pulled back the veil on the other side of Ashoka – the exacting and challenging side. "What would PLAN do with a million dollars?" he asked.

Vickie and I exchanged glances. Bill was going to introduce us to a secret funder. Finally! We started to rattle off our favourite projects, but Bill didn't seem interested. "I don't mean a grant," he interrupted. "I'm talking about leveraging PLAN's financial assets to attract business partners and further your mission."

"How would that work?" I asked, trying not to look too disappointed. "PLAN doesn't have that kind of money."

The rest of the meal was a blur, as Bill introduced us to the emerging world of patient capital, equity financing, social investing and social finance – concepts as unfamiliar and elusive to us as all the foreign languages spoken by Ashoka's international fellows. Bill believes the social enterprise sector can benefit from the private sector's experience of mobilizing resources at scale. His bold ambition is to halt the decline of affordable rental housing in the US for seniors, people with disabilities and low-income families. He retired early from a successful corporate law career to co-found Stewards of Affordable Housing for the Future. A consortium of major affordable housing providers, SAHF collectively owns more than a hundred thousand units. Their daily experience with preserving affordable housing, combined with their critical mass, obliges government to pay attention to the policy solutions they propose. SAHF has also become a major player in the rental market, leveraging their collective housing stock to secure more favourable financing terms. Bill was awarded a Purpose Prize fellowship for creating this unique model of shared ownership, which combines scale, business savvy and social mission.

We left the restaurant with Bill's words ringing in our ears: "We must move away from small-scale silos to collaborations at scale that leverage private, public and philanthropic resources."

If I Had a Million Dollars

The truth was, Vickie and I didn't have an answer to Bill's question. We'd been so busy financing PLAN's day-to-day operation that we'd stopped thinking about our big ideas. We had barely scratched the surface of social entrepreneurship. We were treating social enterprise as an adjunct to fundraising, we realized. Our social enterprise activity was small-scale and divorced from our social objectives. And, as we were soon to discover, we were ignoring the economic assets of our members.

We flew home to PLAN determined to make sense of our delicious confusion. We started a new committee and, to shake things up, we named it "If We Had a Million Dollars" after the Barenaked Ladies song. We brought in advisers from financial institutions to teach us how money works. And we began to take advantage of the opportunities that had been in front of us all along.

We discovered that while the sons and daughters of PLAN members were poor, most of them living on basic disability benefits, their combined disposable income in Canada was $47 billion. The total purchasing power and financial assets (mortgages, savings, investments, business accounts) of their families, friends, service providers and professional supporters could also be mobilized.

Once we adopted this new approach, PLAN began calculating its economic power as follows. One in ten Canadians has a disability. Each of those individuals has at least two others – a relative, friend or professional – who are interested in their well-being. Therefore, at a minimum, at least three in ten Canadians are part of the untapped disability market. PLAN also estimates the number of wills to be written or revised, discretionary trusts to be established and life insurance policies to be taken out. This helps us quantify PLAN's collective spending power when we negotiate partnerships with law firms, insurance companies and financial institutions.

We've learned that the total disposable income of the disability sector in Canada is in excess of $300 billion – and rising, because of aging baby boomers. We are richer than we thought. You and your group are too.

What Colour Is Your Market?

You can accelerate social change by mobilizing your collective net worth. As Dr. Moses Coady, founder of the Coady International Institute and perhaps Canada's greatest community economic developer, suggests in this chapter's opening quotation, we don't need to sit in the economic bleachers. We can flex our economic muscles.

But first we have to appreciate that we have them. That means looking through an "abundance lens:" looking at the spending patterns, combined bank accounts and other financial assets of both your direct membership and your wider constituency of supporters.

While in Europe recently, I heard repeated references to the "grey euro" and the "grey pound" – idioms for the purchasing power of seniors. Once you become aware of companies that cater to the aging market, you see them everywhere. Travel companies and financial institutions immediately come to mind. So does Viagra. So does L'Oréal, which hired Jane Fonda as its new television face. Less obvious are entertainment and communication companies, like Apple and Amazon, that know seniors are major purchasers of their services and products. Did you know Twitter's fastest-growing demographic is the 55–64 age bracket?

You don't have to patronize those companies or agree with their campaigns, but they are capitalizing on a market you might be able to leverage too.

CARP (formerly the Canadian Association of Retired Persons) is certainly doing so. They are becoming a vibrant, effective political voice for seniors. They are establishing business partnerships through Zoomer magazine, and are promoting a new vision of aging in Canada – one that addresses financial security, fair access to health care and freedom from discrimination. CARP knows that seniors own a large majority of the financial assets in this country and that they're the most politically active age group, with the highest voter turnout and most frequent contact with politicians.

CARP is also influencing a much younger generation. Following CARP's lead, for instance, is Generation Squeeze, an organization that represents Canadians under 45. Gen Squeeze is campaigning to secure a "better generational deal" in terms of reducing student debt, saving for a home and finding affordable childcare.

Pink tourism is another lucrative niche market, aimed at the gay and lesbian population. Travel agents, airlines, resorts, cruise lines, and advertising and promotion companies now actively cater to the substantial purchasing power of this community. According to a survey by Tourism Intelligence International, ten percent of international tourists are gay and lesbian, accounting for more than seventy million arrivals worldwide and a $55 billion annual market. The survey found that ninety-four percent of gays and lesbians would go out of their way to buy products and services marketed directly to them.

Accompanying these financial considerations are changing attitudes toward sexual and gender minorities. Think, for example, of the Pride parade. The most recent one in Toronto attracted more than a million people. The fact that celebrities, politicians and police chiefs now participate is a telling barometer for the relationship between changing cultural perceptions and economic power. The Toronto Pride parade alone brings an additional $286 million in direct spending to the Greater Toronto Area.

The green market is also huge. As one example, an advocacy campaign by ForestEthics forced retailer Victoria's Secret to stop using wood fibre from Canada's boreal forest for its publications. The image of a chainsaw-holding lingerie model beneath the headline "Victoria's Dirty Secret" made it easy for the company to do the right thing. This campaign set a new standard for the whole catalogue industry: that it should source its paper from environmentally friendly suppliers.

All groups have a market impact, even the so-called poorest of the poor. In this book's introduction, I discussed the best example of how that particular market is being mobilized. Microcredit, the practice of providing very small loans to people who are poor and don't have the collateral or credit history for a regular bank loan, is one component of an emerging market known as the "bottom of the pyramid." The term refers to the billions of people who live on less than two dollars a day. Bottom-of-the-pyramid thinking asks us to stop seeing the poor as victims and to instead appreciate their entrepreneurship and collective economic power. To date microcredit has benefited more than 80 million people worldwide.

Poor people are natural entrepreneurs, says microcredit pioneer Muhammad Yunus, because their business activities are a matter of survival. Similarly, your survival as a group, and indeed your flourishing, may depend on discovering the colour, size, texture and potential of your market.

Here are some questions that might help you.

- What are the combined economic assets of your membership and constituency? Include any financial resources they receive from government. (Your members are people directly involved in your organization. Your constituency is people who will be affected by the changes you make through business partnerships or government policy.)
- Who else supports your campaign, issue or organization? Companies? Allied professionals? Other organizations? Can you quantify their assets?
- Who are your natural business partners? What products, services, spending patterns and financial assets within your membership may be of value to them?
- What businesses rely on your patronage? Do they invest in the local economy where your members live? Will they hire your members?

Good Money

Mobilizing your economic power to achieve social good is not a new idea. North America's first credit union was established in 1901, in Quebec, by reporter Alphonse Desjardins. He founded the first caisse populaire after learning of a Montrealer ordered to pay nearly $5,000 in interest on a $150 loan. Dr. Moses Coady launched the Antigonish movement during the Depression, igniting a co-operative economy in Nova Scotia that's still going strong. Today 17 million Canadians (4 out of 10) are members of co-ops, credit unions and caisses populaires. Mountain Equipment Co-op, with 3 million members, is the largest retail co-operative in Canada.

This is momentum we can build on.

But first a caveat. As we add business methods to our toolkits, we should not be seduced into thinking they are the solution to all our problems. With some exceptions, modern business has not been a driver for social, economic or environmental justice. Rather, it has produced and exacerbated these challenges. There is a democratic deficit in the corporate structure because a company's primary allegiance is to the shareholder, not the community at large.

An exception is Vancity, Canada's largest credit union, with more than $20 billion in assets and half a million members. Reciprocity, trust and the common good are embedded into the fabric of Vancity's economic relationships. In 2010 Vancity became the first North American credit union to reach carbon neutrality. In 2011 it became the largest organization in Canada to guarantee employees a living wage.

Not content to rest on its laurels, Vancity is now reinventing the credit union model. "We already share thirty percent of our profits with members and communities," president and CEO Tamara Vrooman told me, "in contrast to banks, which might return one percent or two percent to the community and the rest to shareholders." Vrooman is convinced that one of the responsibilities of credit unions in the twenty-first century is to invest differently.

That's why Vancity intends to invest its $20 billion in capital assets to achieve social impact. Vancity calls this commitment "good money." Its new triple bottom line is people, planet and profit. "We see this as a sustainable economic model to drive future business," says Vrooman. She adds, "The better the

community, the better the society, the better our banking business."
And the better banking is in general. In Canada, where Vancity
goes, so do other financial institutions – eventually.

This is the kind of disruption of the traditional business
model that we need. Businesses and corporations can help tackle
social and environmental issues, but to do so, they will have to
move beyond maximizing profit to a triple bottom line similar to
Vancity's.

Power and Money

There are many benefits to harnessing your group's economic power
to achieve social impact.

First, you reduce your dependence on project funding.
Instead, you acquire flexible funds to use on the priorities set by
you, not your funders. Second, you gain new allies who will help
further your mission. PLAN's partnerships with law firms and
financial institutions have generated revenue as well as improved
financial products and services for people with disabilities and their
families. These partners also shaped and supported our Registered
Disability Savings Plan campaign. Third, you're less dependent on
government grants, leaving you free to advocate without fear of
biting the hand that feeds you. Fourth, your impact is amplified.
By blending funding from multiple sources, you create unique
synergies that increase your capacity to spread your innovation.

Finally, there's a psychological benefit – a shift in mindset
from scarcity to abundance, and from victim to agent. Former
PLAN president Joan Lawrence described it this way: "For the first
time as a nonprofit board member, I am no longer on my knees
begging for funds. We can now do our work with our head up
rather than our hand out."

Taking Care of Business: Five Ways to Mobilize Your Economic Power

Entrepreneurial income generated by nonprofits in Canada is already at thirty-five percent of their annual operating budgets. Social entrepreneurship is no longer a marginal pursuit; it's a field in itself.

Social entrepreneurs leverage their resources and assets in two ways. They're either producers, who start a social enterprise or social-purpose business, or consumers, who use their purchasing power for social impact. Here are five examples of what economic mobilization is doing for social innovation.

1. Influencing the Operational Practice of Business

In 2007 *Harry Potter and the Deathly Hallows* became the greenest book in history thanks to choices made about the paper it was printed on. With twenty-five international editions and a print run of twelve million books in the United States alone, that's a lot of old-growth trees left standing.

The catalyst for this decision was Nicole Rycroft and her organization, Canopy. With J. K. Rowling's support, Canopy proved to publishers and book lovers that it was possible to print a blockbuster book without destroying forests in the process. Rycroft, like many environmentalists, has participated in her fair share of protests. She still will if necessary. For instance, she was escorted out of China for unfurling a "Free Tibet" banner during the 2008 Beijing Summer Olympics. But her epiphany came much earlier, during the Clayoquot Sound protests against clear-cut logging on Vancouver Island, at the time the largest act of civil disobedience in Canadian history. Rycroft knew that sooner or later the logging trucks would break through. There had to be a better way to protect fragile forest ecosystems.

Since an estimated ninety percent of logging in Canada is done in old-growth forests, and roughly fifty percent of what's cut goes into making paper, Rycroft decided to influence the purchasing practices of the world's biggest paper suppliers. She now works in the boardroom to secure change in the forest, and she sees business as a powerful distribution system for environmental change.

Today seven hundred of the world's largest paper consumers – including Scholastic, Random House, Hearst, the *Globe and Mail* and Rogers Publishing – have pledged to stop using virgin tree fibre that originates from endangered forests. The Canadian book industry is the greenest on the planet, with seventy-five percent of Canadian book publishers printing up to ninety-five percent of their titles on environmentally sustainable papers. The Canadian industry has sparked an international movement, with green publishing initiatives underway in thirteen other countries.

2. Commercializing Intellectual Property

Just as France is the birthplace of champagne, Ethiopia is the birthplace of coffee. The rituals, aromas and flavours of coffee now integral to everyday life in many parts of the world originated there a thousand years ago. Half the population of Ethiopia is involved in coffee production.

Champagne production is tightly controlled. Producers of bubbly outside France's Champagne region would be sued if they labelled their product "champagne." But the situation is different for Ethiopian coffee. Until New Zealander Ron Layton came along in 2007, Ethiopian farmers received less than five percent of the retail value of the coffee they produced. The export price at the time was a dollar per pound, but retailers were selling coffee for more than twenty dollars a pound in North America, Europe and Japan. Farmers earned only pennies per pound for their labour, expertise and traditional knowledge.

Producers in developing countries rarely benefit from the high retail prices of their best products, even when a product's distinctiveness originates with them. Layton founded Light Years IP to help producers take more control over the distribution of their distinctive products and increase their share of export income. In collaboration with the Ethiopian government, Layton designed and managed the Ethiopian Fine Coffee Trademarking and Licensing Initiative, which trademarked three of the country's finest coffees (Yirgacheffe, Harar and Sidamo) and then licensed distributors – a hundred and twenty to date. Starbucks was the last holdout. Thanks to the International Senior Lawyers Project, an initiative by Bill Kelly, our friend from Ashoka, Layton got pro bono help to negotiate Starbucks' cooperation.

Overall, the intellectual property value capture of the venture Layton started nets an extra $100 million a year for Ethiopian farmers, coffee producers and the country's economy. Now, if they could just get all coffee beverages labelled "Méthode Éthiopienne."

I like the mindset associated with Light Years IP. The social sector invents so many products and services that migrate to the commercial sector without a whiff of acknowledgement, let alone financial compensation. PLAN's social enterprise strategy is based on quantifying our intellectual property – our knowledge of how to support the future planning requirements of people with disabilities and their families. Instead of giving away our expertise, we've made it the basis of our partnerships with law firms and financial institutions. I encourage you to consider your group's intellectual property and to investigate whether it might produce income for your constituency.

3. Nurturing the Sharing Economy

Chris Diplock mixed something old – the concept of a library – with something new – all those home repair, gardening and bicycle maintenance tools you use only once in a while – to create something borrowed: the Vancouver Tool Library. Along the way he reduced waste, saved people money and nurtured neighbourliness. Designed as a co-op, the tool library has more than eight hundred members and a thousand tools in circulation.

Edmonton economist Mark Anielski writes: "Economics is failing humanity, in part, because it has lost touch with the original meaning of the word economy, which from the Greek is concerned with the wise management of the household." Anielski believes the world is on the cusp of a major economic paradigm shift, away from a narrow focus on profits and economic growth (specifically GDP) to one based on optimizing well-being and quality of life.

One sign of this shift is the rise of the sharing economy, which encompasses community gardens, car sharing, couchsurfing, office-sharing hubs, Craigslist, eBay, crowdfunding, Airbnb, second-hand stores, time banks and tool libraries. This phenomenon is also called the gift economy or collaborative consumption. Sometimes money changes hands and sometimes it doesn't.

Sharing, lending, swapping and bartering have been around for a long time. Many attribute their resurgence to technology. Thanks to free open-source software and the omnipresence of the web, a decentralized network of individuals can now operate as seamlessly as a corporation.

Cities are the major beneficiaries of the sharing economy. That's why the McConnell Foundation recently launched Cities for People, a cross-Canada initiative to help cities reap the social, ecological and economic benefits of the sharing economy. These benefits include:

- Local economic development – sharing saves people money. Does everyone really need to own their own extension ladder or car? Local economic development also creates new jobs and promotes new investment.
- Greener cities – car-sharing programs, for example, reduce pollution, the number of cars on the road and the need for parking spaces.
- Civic engagement – sharing is a way of building meaningful connections within a neighbourhood. Says Chris Diplock, "Nothing warms my heart more than seeing an accomplished handyman share his expertise with young people."

4. Purchasing Locally

Coro Strandberg has taken her training as a social work professional into new territory. She pursues her commitment to economic and social justice as Canada's foremost expert on corporate social innovation. Strandberg helped design a Buy Smart program for the Vancouver Organizing Committee for the 2010 Olympic and Paralympic Winter Games. VANOC committed to purchasing goods and services from local businesses and social enterprises, particularly those owned by or employing socially and economically disadvantaged groups.

A recent study by the Centre for Social Innovation and Impact Investing at UBC's Sauder School of Business found that "a local company will recirculate 75-100% more revenue back into the local economy than a multinational company. That means more local jobs, business development and stronger local economies."

Local purchasing is both a bottom-up and a top-down approach to strengthening local markets and achieving social impact. Governments, businesses and nonprofits spend billions annually on goods and services. That's why Coro Strandberg has become a champion of local purchasing and procurement practices. VANOC, for example, spent nearly $60 million to jumpstart Aboriginal businesses in British Columbia and another $1.2 million on jobs for inner-city businesses in Vancouver.

The Buy Smart Program that Strandberg helped design has also become a model for future global sporting events. The 2015 Pan Am/Parapan Am Games in Toronto, as one example, have embedded inclusive purchasing goals into the design of their event.

5. Starting a Social-Purpose Business

There are many branches of PLAN's work. The boldest and most experimental to date is Tyze Personal Networks. As I described under Pattern Two, Tyze's web platform provided the right container for proving the value of personal networks to policy makers.

Another unique aspect of Tyze is its financial structure. Tyze was incorporated by PLAN as a business, albeit a business with a difference. It is a social-purpose business, focused on both economic return and social impact, with PLAN as its largest shareholder.

Vickie created Tyze to get PLAN's network model of care out into the world as quickly as possible. She thought making friends with market forces would help Tyze spread. Businesses and corporations have distribution systems you can piggyback on, thus saving the costs of creating your own. Business investors are also good at measuring financial outcomes. Vickie wanted to use those metrics to add legitimacy to Tyze. Finally, she wanted to take advantage of equity, a source of financing not available to nonprofits, and to see if she could combine it with grants, loans and donations to finance her bold vision.

A social-purpose business is an attempt to transform the traditional business model. It isn't corporate social responsibility or corporate philanthropy. It has twin goals: to make money and to make a difference.

And it is very hard to pull off.

Securing financing for Tyze was much harder than Vickie expected. Traditional nonprofit funders were uncomfortable giving money to a business, regardless of its social objectives. Business investors were nervous, thinking Tyze's social mission would dilute its ability to make them money.

While Tyze's original investors were patient and believed in the social impact the company aspired to, the next round of potential investors proved more hard-nosed. Sadly, traditional business financing wasn't compatible with Tyze's focus on being inclusive, accessible and affordable. When push came to shove, making money outweighed doing good. Tyze's carefully researched and proven social support outcomes didn't count for much, except with a few Canadian foundations. Those foundations were willing to invest their capital based on economic and social objectives.

Vickie has reached the same conclusion as Muhammad Yunus, the microcredit pioneer. He is no longer interested in trying to transform the traditional business model. Now, besides his work on microfinancing, he's introducing a new business structure based on the principles of "no loss" and "no dividend."

Yunus makes his case in the book *Building Social Business: The New Kind of Capitalism That Serves Humanity's Most Pressing Needs*, which includes the example of Grameen Danone, a social business that provides nutritious food to children in Bangladesh. In a social business, all profits are reinvested in the company or in starting another social business. The shareholders get back only their original investment. Yunus thinks this new social business model will appeal to the emerging generation who are not as interested as their predecessors in making profit.

Starting a social-purpose business is not for the faint of heart. Tyze remains the only example in Canada of a business that used social financing to support caregiving.

PLAN's Approach to Social Enterprise

As I noted earlier, PLAN has a natural affinity with law firms, trust and estate-planning companies, life insurance agencies and financial institutions. We're in the same business – helping people plan for their future. Over time we've developed business partnerships with many of these kinds of companies. Our social enterprise pursuits have brought in as much as sixty percent of PLAN'S operating revenue while helping to fulfill our social mission.

PLAN has four criteria for social enterprise initiatives. They must help us:

• achieve our social mission and program goals
• increase the distribution and size of our membership
• add value for our partners
• earn flexible revenue for new ventures

Our longest partnership has been with Vancity. After discovering that PLAN members were twice as likely as the general population to be Vancity members, PLAN and Vancity agreed to explore the emerging disability market together. We agreed to a partnership that gave PLAN a fraction of a percentage of the total amount of funds under administration by our constituency, including their savings and business accounts, mortgages and RRSPs. Constituency was broadly defined as individuals with disabilities along with their families, friends, service providers and supporters.

Everyone won.

Vancity gained a competitive advantage in the emerging disability market. It also strengthened member loyalty and attracted new business, particularly from those associated with people with disabilities. PLAN gave Vancity advice on how to customize existing products and services for the disability market and offered "disability confident" training to Vancity staff.

People with disabilities and their families received better and more competitive services. For example, Vancity waived its membership fees for people with disabilities, and kept its trust fees lower than those of its banking competitors.

PLAN's membership grew as a result of this high-profile and beneficial partnership. And the new revenue source enabled PLAN to underwrite its advocacy and public policy agenda, especially the campaign for the Registered Disability Savings Plan.

Conclusion

Pope Francis wrote in a recent statement on poverty: "Money must serve, not rule!"

The social sector has always acted as an early warning system, pointing out the cracks in our political and economic system and pursuing imaginative solutions. Mobilizing our economic power puts markets in their place, integrating them into the social order, not disembedding them. In the process we gain new allies and new revenue. Mobilizing our economic power strengthens our political clout. And it allows us to work at a scale few of us ever imagined.

Mobilizing Your Economic Power Means:
- Uncovering the force of your market
- Combining your social and economic power
- Building on the momentum of credit unions and the co-operative economy
- Creating a new economy that favours human beings

CHANTIER DE L'ÉCONOMIE SOCIAL: QUEBEC'S SOCIAL ECONOMY

Every jurisdiction has a social economy that touches all of our lives. It focuses on the people we care most deeply about – children, the elderly and those who are sick, infirm, poor or unemployed.

The Canadian nonprofit sector has annual expenditures of $120 billion, representing eight percent of the country's GDP, more than the retail, mining, gas and oil sectors combined. Imagine what the social sector could do if it mobilized its purchasing power. Yet despite its productive nature and its size, it is ignored by every jurisdiction in North America. Except Quebec.

Since the mid-1990s Quebec has mobilized nonprofits, social enterprises, business, labour, government, co-operatives and social movements to create a definable social economy. That economy includes parent-run daycares, food co-ops, home care services, social housing and recycling services.

The organization responsible for coordinating and promoting Quebec's social economy is the Chantier de l'économie social (Task Force on the Social Economy). Its president and executive director, Nancy Neamtan, describes the group as a "network of networks" intent on democratizing the Quebec economy.

Indeed, Quebec's social economy is well on its way to becoming institutionalized. Its members represent between six and seven percent of Quebec's gross national product. They include 10,000 social economy organizations, employing more than 120,000 people along with countless thousands of volunteers. Together their annual revenues account for more than $20 billion. In recognition of the sector's importance, the Quebec government invested $8.4 billion in the social economy between 2003 and 2008 and established a government bureau for the social economy. In 2013 the Quebec National Assembly passed the Social Economy Act.

In contrast to other jurisdictions, where the nonprofit sector is seen as a net drain on the economy, the Quebec government believes the social economy creates jobs, stimulates local and regional economic development, and provides essential social and environmental services.

The social economy is embedded in Quebec's cultural DNA, proving that it's possible to have a vision of an economy based on what matters most to people.

5

ADVOCATE WITH EMPATHY

*Citizenship, if it means anything, means making our desire
for justice active. It is not something we can do alone.*

— Mark Kingwell, The World We Want

"There's no way around it. We'll have to go outside."

It was one of the coldest and stormiest days of the year, which in Ottawa means something – in this case, a wind chill factor of minus thirty. Coming from Vancouver, I hadn't thought to pack a hat, and my scarf wasn't long enough to cover my ears.

"Don't worry," said Sean Moore, the dean of Ottawa lobbyists. "We'll find someplace close. What do you like to eat?"

Jack Styan, PLAN's director of public policy, and I were in town to try to convince yet another cabinet minister to adopt our ideas for a disability savings plan. That meant we'd get fifteen minutes with a ministerial assistant if we were lucky. These meetings were proving as inhospitable as the weather. Then someone suggested Sean Moore might be willing to help.

As we settled into a restaurant booth, Sean laughed. Jack and I were so cold we kept our coats on. "What brings you to town?" he asked. "You're obviously not here for the weather."

Over the meal we explained our multi-tiered proposal. "Okay, I think I get the general picture," Sean said. "Now talk to me as if I'm the minister." When we finished, he asked us if we'd ever heard of strategic inquiry. We hadn't.

Sean started by quoting the Roman statesman Cicero: "If you wish to persuade me, you must think my thoughts, feel my feelings and speak my words." He explained that strategic inquiry is the process of discovering the priorities, language and tools of the group you're trying to convince – in this case, government. "Every person you're trying to influence has a blizzard of material, demands and crises coming at them," Sean continued. "There's intense rivalry for their attention. To be successful, you have to be able to penetrate their overloaded consciousness, to break through the clutter. If you want government to have empathy for your issue, you must have empathy for their challenges."

Jack and I nodded, certain we were already doing what he suggested. But Sean, the epitome of a true gentleman, wasn't convinced. He asked if he could level with us. "I didn't understand most of what you said a moment ago. I suspect the minister won't either. You've got too many ideas, and they don't align with government priorities. I don't think you're ready to meet him."

It was the start of a beautiful relationship.

Both Sides Now

In her book *Systems of Survival*, Jane Jacobs explains that the nature of government is inherently conservative. Government's job is to preserve what exists, even if what it's preserving is unjust or outdated. Jacobs calls the collection of habits, traits and norms associated with government the guardian syndrome. Loyalty, tradition, obedience, discipline and honour are some of the most highly prized values of this syndrome. Government's structures and processes – its bureaucracies and policy making – are not set up for overnight change. Hierarchy, fear of precedent and caution are built into government's DNA. This has many benefits, but it has drawbacks too.

That's the broad context for public policy work. On top of that, governments today are expected to do more with less, to increase productivity as resources decline. As citizens we want government to anticipate problems and prevent them before they arise. At the same time, governments must respond to a sophisticated citizenry that expects government to keep pace with the technologies, choices, standards and personalized services we encounter in the private sector. We want our public services to be as responsive and as tailored as Netflix, but at no extra cost.

Unfortunately, our expectations of creativity and flexibility coexist in a political environment where government is risk-averse, ever more attentive to short-term priorities, under intense media scrutiny and subject to a disproportionate focus on accountability and transparency. It's no wonder good ideas fight for a foothold.

Just when we need it most, the public sector's capacity to innovate is constrained. Innovative politicians and public servants scarcely have room to manoeuvre. Yes, our government institutions are imperfect; the people who inhabit them know that as well as anyone else. The point is, government may not be able to do much about it.

That's the job of citizens, as Mark Kingwell's statement at the beginning of this chapter suggests. If a certain degree of government paralysis has set in, then citizens and advocates need to figure out a way to accommodate government's limitations and improve how it functions. That's what we'd do if a friend had a spinal cord injury.

Solution-Based Advocacy

We need government, regardless of who is in power. Their track record and our previous disappointment with their unresponsiveness or callousness don't really matter. We are they. They are we.

Laws, regulations, policy, taxation, contracting, procurement, setting and enforcing standards, reallocating resources – these are all indispensable tools for achieving impact. So is government's distribution system, which is second to none. The government is in contact with everyone. We need government at its innovative best, particularly if we want its representatives to fulfill their roles as receptive social innovators.

That's why a new breed of advocates is emerging, who support more innovation and risk-taking within government. These people are proponents of solution-based advocacy. They have two objectives: to propose solutions and to enhance government's capacity to make better decisions.

Solution-based advocates want to do more than oppose government or focus unduly on what's not working. They're tired of reacting, and they work hard to cultivate a proactive mindset. Their focus is on workable solutions. These folks haven't gone soft, parking their issues until government gets its act together. Neither are they naive. They are prudent. They want results, just like everyone else, but they also want to improve relationships among all the players, to attract new allies, to build a base for addressing the next set of challenges.

Perhaps where solution-based advocates differ most from traditional lobbyists is in their focus on means as well as ends. They recognize that jamming something through a system doesn't usually work, because the system's culture doesn't change. If anything, it becomes more defensive.

Solution-based advocates bring empathy to their work. In doing so, they:

- strengthen relationships while seeking solutions
- accept that there are no easy answers to our toughest challenges
- create the conditions for joint problem solving
- understand that the vast majority of issues are not "either/or" or "we/they" but lie in the grey area between
- commit to sorting out competing principles and values, rather than leaving that role exclusively to government
- practise civility and respect, addressing the problem, not the character of the individuals involved

Five Characteristics of Solution-Based Advocacy

Solution-based advocacy is not an easy road to follow. Governments may not respond in kind. Colleagues and allies may not be supportive. Some people will accuse you of having sold out. It's much easier to assume you are right and move with force. It's much harder to heed Martin Luther King's words: "…all life is interrelated. Somehow we are tied in a single garment of destiny, caught in an inescapable network of mutuality, where what affects one directly affects all indirectly…."

Nevertheless, solution-based advocates are filling the gaps left by government. They are breaking apart logjams and creating partnerships with unlikely allies, including politicians and civil servants who want to take risks and try out innovative ideas. Like everyone else in the social innovation space, these advocates are blurring traditional roles and responsibilities.

Here are five approaches today's solution-based advocates are taking to their work.

1. Searching for a Heart of Gold

I have a confession to make. When Stephen Harper was first elected prime minister, I turned to Vickie and said, "I think I'm falling a little in love with him."

She wasn't surprised. I fall a little in love with politicians, regardless of their political affiliation, all the time. I no longer treat them as targets or objects to be manipulated. Instead, I warm to them, looking for points of connection.

I do it for a couple of reasons. Most of them are decent people who get into politics to make a difference. Sure, they're a little larger than life, but you have to project in the political arena or you won't get elected. Also, I'm inclined to agree with Goethe's confession that he could see no fault committed that he might not have committed himself. The egos, foibles and imperfections of politicians remind me that I too am a mixture of good and bad qualities.

I imagine sharing a late-night whisky with politicians or going for a bike ride with them while talking about desire, kids or destiny. I become interested in who they are, not what they do. It's not that our differences don't matter. But their potential – what they can be and should be – matters more.

I've lost my edge, according to some people. Don't I realize that this party has a master plan to destroy our country, that this particular politician is incompetent and that one is a buffoon? My detractors conveniently forget that political life is strewn with broken promises. One politician's cunning is another's grand design. And beneficial policy can come from unlikely sources. Few at the time thought Brian Mulroney would gain a reputation as our greenest prime minister. My critics also appear to have little faith in the long-standing resilience of our democratic institutions which endure despite what any one government does.

I live and breathe public policy advocacy, both directly and as a coach. I spend as much time on mindset as I do on strategy. Certain ways of thinking can derail good intentions. Righteous indignation is one. It makes us more angry than effective. Absolute certainty is another. We become smug about our solutions, more focused on being right (or being seen to be right) than on being open to alternatives. We demonize those who disagree with us. We ignore the ethical complexity of issues, refusing to accept that there may be no easy solution.

Another trap is treating government as the enemy. When we do that, we adopt the methods of opposition parties, denouncing and criticizing, blaming and polarizing.

Still another way to get off track is to be seduced by political drama and scandal. I like intrigue as well as the next person, but it is a distraction. Dramas and scandals reduce government risk taking, the very thing we want to encourage. They also breed cynicism about politicians and the political process. Getting rid of a rogue politician or a governing party may be necessary, but it doesn't address the reality that our biggest social and environmental challenges transcend partisan allegiances and political mandates.

2. Using Strategic Inquiry

After our initial meeting with Sean Moore, Jack and I kept in touch with him. We did our best to follow his advice and adapt our material, and we made some headway. A disability savings plan had become a plank in Prime Minister Paul Martin's 2006 election platform. But Martin's Liberals lost the election. We were certain that years of work had been wiped out. We didn't know what to do.

A few months into the new Conservative government's mandate, CBC national news profiled the remarkable life and last days of David Cohen, one of PLAN's earliest lifetime members. David, a classical music lover and human rights activist, had died of brain cancer. The documentary touched everyone's heart, including Sean's. He called the next morning.

"How are you coming with your savings plan idea, Al?" he asked.

I explained our worry that the fingerprints of the defeated Liberal government were all over the concept. We didn't think there was any way the new government would take it on.

"I wouldn't be so sure," he replied. "Let's try a little strategic inquiry."

Sean coached us well. We stopped peddling our preferred solution and instead focused on the challenges faced by individuals and families. As far as solutions went, we simply said we imagined something like an RRSP or an RESP. That seemed to be enough – more than enough, because the final version of the RDSP was significantly better than our original proposal.

Strategic inquiry is a prelude to more active lobbying. It's based on the premise that the best way to learn about the procedures, language and priorities of those you're trying to influence is to ask them. It's important to listen carefully and not talk too much. As a rule, you should spend eighty percent of the time receiving and only twenty percent broadcasting. You can sketch your big idea in general terms but should resist the impulse to get into details. Your job is to gain an understanding of government's stated and unstated objectives.

There are many benefits to strategic inquiry. Among them are the key information you gather about government themes and priorities, the relationships you make, the credibility you establish and the champions you discover. In PLAN's case we learned Jim Flaherty, the newly appointed federal finance minister, had a son with a disability. When I eventually met Minister Flaherty in 2008, it was clear he deeply understood the purpose behind our disability savings plan proposal. As you might expect, an important byproduct of strategic inquiry is the chance to educate government about your issue even while you're seeking advice.

It's hard enough to influence governments' existing priorities. It's even harder to convince them to set another priority. Strategic inquiry gives you the feedback to refine and reframe your proposal. It helps you shape a realistic question that will be seen to advance both your agenda and government's. At the very least your existing proposal will be sharpened. You may discover there's more than one way to achieve your objective. Or you might modify your proposal now that you better understand the political and public service environment. And because you're educating people about your issue, you increase the chances they might do something about it.

3. Cultivating a Network of Champions

Solution-based advocacy focuses on relationships. People are more likely to say yes to someone they know and trust. There are allies attached to every system, at every level, who are waiting for a good idea and the right person to come along. It's important to cultivate an informal network of champions that includes politicians, political advisers and public servants, as well as business and community leaders and, potentially, celebrities.

Don Lenz is one of the many members of PLAN's expanded network of support. He's an investment banker in Toronto. In 2005, at the annual meeting of a private foundation, which he chaired, Don heard Vickie explain how PLAN lifetime member Gordon Walker's passion for horses led him out of isolation into a life rich with friends. Don asked whether Vickie and I would be willing to meet with him and his brother, whose daughter had a disability, next time we were in Toronto.

Introductions were barely necessary. We shared the challenges faced by all parents who have sons and daughters with disabilities: the fight for services and the anxiety about our children's future well-being. Our connection with Don's brother was instant and deep, as it often is among parents. When we shared our idea for a disability savings plan, his eyes lit up. "That would be a big help," he said.

Don listened quietly, saying very little during the meeting. As we got up to leave, he made us an offer. "A good friend of mine is on the executive of the Conservative Party of Canada. Should they ever form the government, I'd be happy to introduce you."

Soon after the 2006 election of the Conservatives, Don arranged for Jack Styan and me to meet in Ottawa with someone he described only as a "senior Conservative strategist." Her office was at the back of a deserted hall filled with rows of desks, banks of computers, phones, whiteboards, flipcharts, discarded coffee cups and lots of Conservative posters. We realized we were in Conservative election headquarters, or what politicos call the war room.

Our strategist was surprisingly familiar with the issues faced by people with disabilities and their families. She had started a local infant development program, and her husband worked in special education. What's more, she had worked on every one of Jim Flaherty's election campaigns. She quickly grasped the disability savings plan concept.

She made one brief, cryptic phone call while we were there. "You know that matter we talked about," we heard her say. "I'll be right over with more details." Turning back to Jack and me, she simply said, "Leave it with me."

We left as puzzled as we were hopeful. Two months went by without any news, and the strategist wasn't returning our calls. Just before Flaherty brought down his first budget, she phoned to suggest it would be a good idea for us to watch the news. Sure enough, the budget declared the federal government's intention to establish a disability savings plan. Jack and I never found out whom the strategist had called, but we have our suspicions it was the minister himself.

4. Solving Problems Together

From 2003 to 2008 Peter Shergold was, as secretary to the PM and Cabinet, Australia's most powerful public servant. During a recent speaking tour of Canada, Peter told me how difficult it had been, even from that position of power, to make bold changes to the structure of democratic governance. Innovation in public service today, Peter said, is preoccupied with efficiency and internal administrative procedures. He believes the way out of this situation is a more authentic collaboration among the sectors.

I've had many conversations with politicians and public servants who agree. They realize government must shift from doing "for" to doing "with." This means that citizens, far from being bystanders, must be meaningfully engaged. Some have labelled this new approach to public policy development "co-creation."

PLAN learned the importance of co-creation when the RDSP was being implemented. Ten provincial and three territorial governments needed to adjust their disability benefit policies to correspond to what the federal government was awarding. That's a lot of moving parts. Some provinces weren't sure what to do. Others clearly intended to claw back the federal contributions, nullifying the benefits to people with disabilities. Federal public servants expressed their concern to PLAN but were in no position to intervene in areas under provincial or territorial jurisdiction.

Sensing that a patchwork of different regulations was going to emerge, PLAN took a leap. We hosted our own federal, provincial and territorial meeting and, to our surprise, most social service ministries sent a representative. Working together, we were able to fashion a consensus about the value of permitting people with disabilities to accumulate assets. The progressive provinces in attendance inspired the others to follow suit.

So successful was the first meeting that PLAN was asked to host another. We had unwittingly created a forum in which federal, provincial and territorial colleagues could meet without the usual formality of such conferences. In the end, all provinces and territories save one eliminated clawback provisions on RDSP assets.

David Mitchell, president and CEO of the Ottawa-based Public Policy Forum, believes that the public servant of the future "will be a relationship manager, able to build and coordinate complex partnerships… among all levels of government and other sectors." To get there, government will have to do many of the same things business and communities are already doing. These include:

- breaking down silos within the public service that prevent cooperation among departments or jurisdictions
- making room for policy experimentation, rapid prototyping and risk taking
- becoming proficient at innovative collaboration with citizens

The transformation of government's role from parent to partner won't happen overnight. One catalyst may be the high number of senior public servants who are retiring and won't easily be replaced. Another may be government's willingness to admit that many of their programs aren't working, no matter how much money they allocate. Sooner or later governments will reach the same conclusion that Canada's former auditor general, Sheila Fraser, reached about First Nations funding:

> I find it really tragic that after ten years, over thirty audits of first nations issues on reserves, a fair bit of money and hard work by public servants, conditions are worse today than ten years ago…We can't keep doing things the same way. Obviously it's just not working.

5. Doing It Themselves

Many advocates don't realize that the political and bureaucratic terrain has changed, and that government's capacity to receive and implement good ideas has been curtailed. According to Sean Moore, advocates now have to do a lot more of the heavy lifting if they want to advance their issues in a timely manner and increase their chances of success. To move your issue along, you may have to take the lead and do it yourself.

Since the 1990s most governments in Canada have eliminated or reduced their policy shops. They no longer employ people to scan the landscape of changing needs, identify emerging challenges, research new approaches and anticipate policy issues.

Advocates who expect government to act on their solutions may be dealing with people who aren't aware there's a problem in the first place and who are swamped with other priorities besides.

Tim Draimin is the driving force behind Canada's social finance agenda. After identifying government roadblocks that needed to come down to allow social entrepreneurs and innovators to flourish, Tim decided the best way to secure action was to create a national task force on social finance. He wanted the federal government to co-sponsor it.

In early 2010 Tim asked if I would arrange a meeting with Jim Flaherty, the finance minister, to propose the idea. I'd worked with Minister Flaherty during the implementation phase of the RDSP and had come to know him. We invited Sean Moore to accompany us.

Unfortunately, the minister declined the invitation for his ministry to co-sponsor the task force. "Your ideas are promising, but look what I've got to deal with," he said, showing us a thick file his officials had prepared. "This file is full of arguments against changing the rules to allow charities to become more entrepreneurial. It's going to take a long time to bring my public service officials along. I can't fight that battle right now. You'll have to proceed without us, but please keep me informed."

We left disappointed. As we were going down in the elevator, Sean asked, "So what are you going to do next?" Simultaneously Tim and I replied, "We'll just have to do it ourselves."

The Canadian Task Force on Social Finance proceeded without government involvement. It made seven recommendations to free up additional resources and to create an enabling tax and regulatory environment for nonprofits and social enterprises. We returned to Ottawa in December 2010 to give Flaherty a personal copy.

To our surprise, he'd already read the report. "Thank you," he said. "You've expedited this agenda. It's something we couldn't do ourselves." As we were leaving, he asked for extra copies. It turned out he was hosting a federal-provincial finance meeting the next weekend. "I'd like to personally give a copy to every provincial minister of finance and their deputy," he said.

Raise a Little Hell

Sometimes governments don't listen, or they bully their way forward. Often we have to do something dramatic to get their attention.

Environmental economist Mark Jaccard was arrested in 2012 for blocking a train carrying US coal destined for Asia via Vancouver's seaport. In "The Accidental Activist," a piece for *The Walrus* magazine, he describes his career helping governments around the world design policies to reduce carbon pollution. Then came the elimination of the National Round Table on the Environment and the Economy, of which Mark was a member. That was followed by layoffs of government scientists, government attacks on environmental groups, and the "streamlining" of environmental review processes, which would accelerate coal port expansion in Vancouver.

Mark writes:

> Albert Einstein once said, "Those who have the privilege to know have the duty to act." We know the climate scientists are right. We know we have a propensity to delude ourselves for reasons of self-interest and convenience, even when the outcome may be devastating. And we know that our government is not owning up to the contradiction between its climate promises and its aggressive effort to expand fossil fuels. If citizens do not act to create a new policy window, effective policies will not happen.

Each of us has a line in the sand. I've blocked roads, sued government, hired undercover operatives and choreographed media events to draw attention to the warehousing of people with disabilities. Mark's line, as he describes it, is "trying to answer the people who forty years from now will surely ask us, 'What did you do when there was still time to make a difference?'"

I've met Mark, though I don't know him well. What I predict is that he, like other activists, accidental or otherwise, will eventually want to get back to the table with government. Getting the system's attention is a prologue. Sooner or later we have to walk through the door and sit down with our opponents. That's when the hard work of shifting our political and economic priorities begins.

Conclusion

Former prime minister Joe Clark calls the symbiotic relationship between civil society and government a marriage between imagination and mandate. What non-governmental organizations don't have, he says, is "the authority to change the rules . . . Non state organizations often have the imagination which the world needs, but only states and governments have the mandate and power to change laws and regulations and obligations."

Democratic governments are works in progress. We live in an era when their imperfections are obvious and their response is slower and more cumbersome than the challenges facing us.

Governments seem stuck. Designed for the machine era, they appear out of place in our digital world. They need our help.

Advocating with Empathy Means:
- Understanding government, not ridiculing or ignoring it
- Following Martin Luther King's advice and conducting ourselves "on the high plane of dignity and discipline"
- Refreshing our democratic institutions

THE REPRESENTATION AGREEMENT ACT: TRIUMPH AND FAILURE

Culture is what you do when no one's looking over your shoulder. It's a slow-moving, formidable, yet largely invisible variable. It's the elephant in the room – with a memory. And we are playing teeter-totter with it.

Cultural change is lasting change. A successful campaign, new law or pool of funds won't achieve its purpose unless we pay attention both to the assumptions of the organizational culture responsible for its implementation and to wider societal beliefs.

A good example of what not to do comes from my participation in the British Columbia Adult Guardianship Coalition in the late 1980s and early 1990s. The coalition, which comprised over three hundred grassroots groups and activists, as well as professionals and their associations, aimed to modernize adult guardianship legislation. We established a joint working committee with the BC government and the office of the BC public guardian.

The purpose of adult guardianship is to protect vulnerable people from being exploited while honouring their choices. It's common practice for guardianship legislation to define incompetence based solely on mental ability. Many of us in the coalition believed this should not be the only criterion for determining a person's decision-making competence. We knew from experience that a trusting, mutually supportive relationship keeps people safe and helps them to make decisions. We wanted the legal definition of capacity to be expanded to reflect what we described as interpersonal intelligence or social competence.

Our proposal to expand the definition of legal capacity was very challenging for lawyers, doctors and hospital administrators. It wasn't part of their training or experience. They thought it would be much harder to quantify than the existing concept of mental capacity. And we didn't realize we were taking on a common-law definition of mental capacity that was centuries old.

In 1993, after six years of lobbying, BC's Representation Agreement Act was passed. The act enabled people who would traditionally be deemed incompetent to determine who they wanted to support them to make decisions. This included many seniors as well as people with disabilities, brain injuries and mental illness. The act included a new criterion for determining a person's legal competence: the existence of relationships characterized by trust. No such criterion exists in adult guardianship legislation anywhere else.

The campaign had been hard fought, but it was finally over. Or so we thought.

Two years passed. The law was not proclaimed, which meant it couldn't be implemented. In the meantime our coalition splintered into factions. Most of the community advocates were on one side; most of the lawyers and health administrators were on the other. Old hostilities and suspicions resurfaced.

I recall a key meeting with two influential members of the BC bar association. Our delegation walked into the room overconfident, perhaps a little smug. From the community perspective, we had goodness on our side and the proof was in the new legislation. The bar association wanted to talk about the potential abuse and exploitation of vulnerable people. We knew they wanted to add safeguards that we felt would undermine the intent of the new legislation.

Before they could finish their opening remarks, one of us interrupted: "The changes are here to stay, and you had better get used to it!" The meeting deteriorated from there. We might as well have said, "Forget your training, your experience, your concerns and three hundred years of legal tradition. We're right. You're wrong."

I ran into one of the lawyers in the washroom after the meeting. He was still fuming. "I could live with the new definition of legal capacity," he admitted, "but I'll be damned if I'll be bullied by those self-righteous so-and-sos. I'm going to fight this."

The die was cast, a potential ally lost, a formidable adversary engaged. As he prophesied, there have been several attempts since then to repeal parts of the Representation Agreement Act.

Our coalition was driven by strategic objectives, and we often stormed over our opposition or relied on shaky compromises. We didn't realize how many permutations and combinations of relationships existed inside the various legal, medical, government, social service and community systems. We didn't realize how ingrained behaviour is, how many hidden places of authority existed, how challenging our new definition of capacity was and how long an adjustment period it would take. Ironically, our own relationships with one another were not characterized by trust.

The controversy over representation agreements has settled. But it has taken its toll. Some of the agreements' powers have been weakened. There is a controversial aura around them. As a result, this low-cost grassroots alternative to formal adult guardianship has not realized its full potential. It will take an injection of advocating with empathy for that to happen.

PATTERN

6

WHO IS AS IMPORTANT AS HOW

....

We were meant I think to be in a state of wonder. Wonder, and
a state of abject humility at the same time.

– John Mighton, interview in *The Varsity Magazine*

Bill Gale had walked by the same man asking for money on the street dozens of times. This time was different. Perhaps it was because Bill had just submitted his retirement letter and was more tuned in to uncertainty and his own vulnerability. Or perhaps the previous Sunday's sermon was still fresh in his mind. Regardless, he stopped and asked to hear the man's story. What he learned provided the spark and the fuel for a successful poverty reduction strategy in Saint John, New Brunswick.

The stranger was a gentle man with a kind face, and Bill understood that his story was essentially about dignity. Injured in a logging accident, the man had lost much, but he still wanted to support his family. "Like me," Bill said, "he was searching for some meaning in his life. He wanted to contribute. I knew I could rally my friends and business colleagues around that."

As a senior bank executive, Bill had done business with the movers and shakers in New Brunswick's establishment for decades. After his fateful encounter he personally invited them to form the Business Community Anti-Poverty Initiative and to make fighting poverty a community priority. Most accepted. Since its founding in 1997, BCAPI has become a key player in a robust, multi-sector partnership aimed at breaking the intergenerational cycle of poverty throughout New Brunswick.

Vickie and I went to interview Bill expecting to gain insight into how to partner with businesses and corporations. Instead, we got a lesson in humility.

"It's true that when businesspeople speak, government tends to pay attention," he said. "But that's not enough." Bill then explained the obvious. He and his colleagues, being among the richest people in New Brunswick, are the least qualified to understand poverty. "Rather than assume we know what's best for people who are poor, we've decided we can be most helpful by listening and observing," Bill told us. "There are enough doers out there. We can be most helpful by keeping our eyes on the forest."

BCAPI focuses on break-the-cycle solutions, particularly those that address intergenerational poverty. By the time we met Bill, his organization was playing a pivotal role in convincing government to address how poverty affects teenage mothers. That included increasing childcare support and helping moms stay in school.

What's happening in New Brunswick is a phenomenon that Vickie and I continue to observe. People who never saw themselves as social change leaders are stepping up. And they want to do more than tinker. They are less certain about solutions, more willing to learn. As an organization, BCAPI commits to learning as much from those who live in poverty as from reports or studies. That has led to a profound shift in their understanding.

In one instance, after hearing from a single mother how a proposed sixteen percent utility rate increase would affect her limited budget, BCAPI appealed the decision to New Brunswick Power. The intervention successfully reversed the rate increase for all people on fixed incomes.

Bill's open heart opened his mind that day he spoke to the stranger on the street. All of sudden poverty had a face. It was no longer an issue he could walk away from. Leaders like Bill Gale are emerging everywhere. Their personal involvement is less about charity and pity and more about recognizing their common humanity with those in distress.

Who they are is just as important as having all the answers.

You Are the One

"How?" can be a killer question. It can stop you dead in your tracks. One way to undermine a new initiative or stop someone from pursuing a big idea is to ask them how they're going to do it. How dampens the imagination and favours being practical far too early. How might have stopped Bill Gale, and prevented a banker from becoming a poverty activist.

Peter Block, author of *The Answer to How Is Yes*, suggests we declare a moratorium on questions beginning with "how." He says that asking how sends us on a search for tools, technology and data and "deflects us from accepting our humanity, our limitations, the fact that the questions that trouble us are inherent in being human and have no real answers." More cruelly, how can imply that because you don't have the answer, there must be something wrong with you for pursuing foolish dreams.

Of course the question of how is important, but it shouldn't dominate. You can teach people techniques. You can give them tools. But you can't teach character. The journey to reconcile the spiritual dimension of our lives with our day-to-day lives is unique and personal.

"Who?" is a life-affirming question. It assumes everyone cares and is capable of making the world a better place. It is inclusive. The price of admission isn't your talent or achievements but your character. Think of a leader you admire, then describe who they are. Chances are you'll describe qualities of character and conviction. Those people have other talents, but that's not what attracts you to them. Intelligence, observed French philosopher, activist and mystic Simone Weil, is enlightened by love.

If the answer to how is yes, then the answer to yes is you.

The Watchman's Gone

The Quakers of the seventeenth century thought of themselves as "God's ordinaries." They meant ordinary in the sense that extraordinary acts are not reserved for the special few – that we are all born with the capacity to be brave, to speak out and to step up.

Today's leaders don't fit the traditional capital "L" view of leadership. They're not just the people at the front of the room, the top of the pyramid or the head of the parade. They embody attributes we associate with leadership – vision, boldness, tenacity and moral character – but they are moving beyond traditional roles, expertise and divisions of labour.

The eruption of small "l" leadership is confusing to those who still rely on the concept of the charismatic leader. The Aung San Suu Kyis and Nelson Mandelas of this world will always inspire us. Yet as majestic as their presence may be, they have never achieved grand results on their own. The absence of their equivalent doesn't mean that our movement or cause is doomed or that we should wait for a capital "L" leader to arrive. We are not "leader-less," suggests Bill McKibben, founder of 350.org. Instead, we are entering a "leader-full" era, when people take their cues from each other rather than from those stuck up front.

There are many people without degrees, official mandates or the ability to attract fanfare who shimmer with passion. They are waiting for the rest of us to look around, to appreciate them and to link up. A resurrection of the ordinary implies recognition of ordinary people and their extraordinary power.

Fumbling toward Ecstasy

The individuals Vickie and I met during our two-year exploration of social innovation are impressive collaborators, communicators, conveners, entrepreneurs and strategists. They know how to get things done.

But they are more than talented doers. We discovered two other common threads. There is a spiritual dimension to the lives of these innovators, and they pay attention to their blind spots or limitations.

Moral Oxygen

Social change can be harsh and unyielding work. It can take a toll on you, your family, your friends, your colleagues and your adversaries.

The sustenance for this journey comes from what Quebec philosopher Jacques Dufresne describes as "moral oxygen." Our bodies can't exist without oxygen. Our souls need similar nourishment. Just as we must protect the air we breathe from contamination, so we must protect the source of our moral oxygen.

Otherwise, we are vulnerable to heartache, burnout, addiction or cynicism. The loss of the soul is painless, Dufresne warns. He advises that we pay attention to what nourishes and replenishes us.

Nowadays people are committed to becoming more peaceful, joyful and happy while pursuing social change. They no longer want to live a divided life. They practise meditation, yoga or tai chi. Others prefer gardening, dancing, walking or, in my case, cycling.

Jean Vanier, philosopher and founder of L'Arche, suggests that it is fundamentally about belonging:

> The longer we journey on the road to inner healing and wholeness, the more the sense of belonging grows and deepens. The sense is not just one of belonging to others and to a community. It is a sense of belonging to the universe, to the earth, to the air, to the water, to everything that lives, to all humanity.

From Hubris to Humility

At a social innovation seminar I attended, a senior government manager said that she oversaw seven hundred programs that support First Nations families living off-reserve in her province. Yet living conditions were getting worse. "We don't need a another program until we figure out what's wrong," she said. "We know we have to do something, but we don't know what it is."

That is humility.

As I write this, a report just released notes that more than $60 million has been spent on a government strategy to support children in care. Yet despite good intentions, talented people and everyone's best efforts, not a single child was directly served.

The most common response after such a catastrophe is to find someone to blame – the participants, the service providers, the bureaucrats, the previous administration or the "system." Then we reorganize, reshuffle and regroup. Some of the players may change, but our approaches seldom do. We think we can figure it out with just one more tweak, or that our solution is "the one" despite what has been tried before, despite what else is going on.

That is hubris.

Hubris refers to people who are overconfident and who overestimate their competency and capabilities. It refers to those who prefer the familiar even when it isn't working, and who are afraid to admit they don't have all the answers. Social entrepreneur Margaret Heffernan associates hubris with willful blindness.

To admit your uncertainty and doubt, as the government manager working with First Nations communities did, requires a shift in mindset from hubris to humility. Humility is an awareness of how much you know and, as a result, of how much more you don't know. It's the recognition that there are no shortcuts and that rigour, focus and time are needed to achieve impact.

Humility doesn't stop you from acting. It does, however, make you more curious, more willing to consider other perspectives and ideas and try other ways.

Five Characteristics of Social Innovators on the Journey to Wholeness

People who are committed to integrating their inner, spiritual dimensions with their outer lives as innovators cultivate five main characteristics.

1. Emotional Maturity

"BREATHE!" That was the only word on the note slipped in front of the lead environmental negotiator.

The Great Bear Rainforest discussions with forest companies were at a crucial stage. Colleagues could sense that the lead negotiator was about to overreact to a careless remark from the other side. The prompt worked. A pause and a deep breath reminded her of the bigger picture and the harm that might come from inflaming the situation.

After years of intense conflict, complex negotiations, media backlash and the occasional death threat, the Great Bear campaigners realized they needed to pay more attention to their emotional and spiritual well-being. Their motivation, according to campaigner Darcy Riddell, "was grounded in the belief that our own state of being and consciousness was affecting the perspectives of our adversaries and the outcomes of our campaign efforts." Several campaigners had started working with the musician and leadership coach Robert Gass on loving kindness meditation, non-violent communication, practising detachment, and visualizing consensus amid contentious discussions.

Conflict and tension are inevitable for change makers. If we don't take care, those outer pressures will seep inside us. Darcy Riddell believes that social innovators must become as intentional about personal and interpersonal transformation as they are about systems change. In an assessment of the final Great Bear Rainforest Agreement, Riddell and her co-authors note that allies and opponents alike believed that the personal transformation undergone by environmental leaders "gave rise to new relationships and laid the groundwork for system transformation." In fact, Riddell believes that the work itself became a "crucible for personal development and transformation."

2. Voice and Agency

Writer and editor Shari Graydon's collection *I Feel Great about My Hands: And Other Unexpected Joys of Aging* profiles forty-one powerful women over fifty. One, then Canadian senator Sharon Carstairs, described how as a young child she had been sexually abused by a family friend, who effectively silenced her by insisting that no one would believe her if she spoke about his violations. Yet in the face of her abuser's developing interest in her younger sister, she found her voice. The act of speaking up to protect another was a pivotal moment that awakened Carstairs' capacity to make change. It was a true act of courage.

The word "courage" is derived from the French word coeur. It means the ability to stand by one's heart or one's core. Courageous people are brave-hearted. Moral courage is not about being fearless, says Aung San Suu Kyi. "Fearlessness may be a gift but perhaps more precious is the courage… that comes from cultivating the habit of refusing to let fear dictate one's actions, courage that could be described as 'grace under pressure.'"

When Sharon Carstairs found her voice, it set her on a path that led far beyond protecting her younger sister, to a lifetime of advocacy and public service. Strength and confidence come from looking fear in the face. Then you will be able to declare, as Sharon Carstairs did, "I feel great about my voice – and about using it!"

3. Intuition

Most disruptive innovators have a capacity to sense an emerging reality and to act in harmony with it. They answer yes to the unbidden.

Donald MacPherson, the community organizer behind Vancouver's four pillars drug strategy (discussed under Pattern Two), worked for ten years at the corner of Main and Hastings, the crossroads of the city's drug trade. For ten years he was surrounded by death, grief, desperation, feeble efforts. He was overwhelmed. One day he read about a safe injection site in Zurich and decided to check it out in person. "I just got a feeling," he told me. "Reading about it wasn't good enough."

Going wasn't easy. Donald's employer, the City of Vancouver, gave him time off with pay, but he had to pay his own way to Europe. "I went over on my sister's free air points," he laughed.

Donald described himself as firing on ninety-eight percent intuition during this period. "I grokked it," he said, borrowing novelist Robert Heinlein's term from *Stranger in a Strange Land.* "It clicked, going to Europe. I could see there was hope. I remember thinking, oh my God, this is dead simple."

Vickie had a similar experience at the birth of Tyze. When Alexandra Samuel and Rob Cottingham, founders of the social media company Social Signal, suggested that PLAN's face-to-face networks could be transformed into a web platform, Vickie felt as if she was bathed in a white light, with every cell in her body vibrating yes. Even though she knew nothing about running a high-tech startup, she knew she had no choice but to pursue their suggestion. And so Tyze began.

4. Patience

John Mighton is as complex and multi-layered as his award-winning play *Half Life*. As a playwright, mathematician, philosopher and social entrepreneur, he embodies a rare blend of the artistic and the scientific. When not writing plays, he's catalyzing a numeracy movement through his organization JUMP (Junior Undiscovered Math Prodigies). Known as Canada's math conscience, Mighton is changing how all of us, but particularly children, are taught math.

Malcolm Gladwell, in his book *Outliers*, argues that it takes ten thousand hours of testing and practising to achieve mastery in a field. John Mighton is a good example of the meticulousness and patience required of all social innovators. It took him years to solidify his insights and perfect his approach. As he writes in *The End of Ignorance*:

> It wasn't until I read Sylvia Plath's letters to her mother and saw how as a teenager she had learned her craft in small, determined steps, dismantling poems like motors to see how they worked and writing imitations of the things she loved, that I began to believe there was a path I could follow to develop a voice of my own.

Though JUMP's method of guided discovery is becoming part of the math curriculum in school systems around North America and Britain, Mighton knows that tackling misconceptions about ability is just the beginning. His experience reminds us that the time required for a social innovation to have impact can't be measured in hours or even years, but rather in decades or half-lifetimes.

One theme of Mighton's play *Half Life* is interruption – the idea that humans are at the mercy of forces we can't control. Our lives are shaped by constant interruptions, trivial pursuits, accidents and innumerable small steps that lead to the occasional breakthrough.

Regrettably, the solutions to our toughest problems can't be hurried. We must resign ourselves to a terrible paradox: being patient despite the urgency of the crises we see around us.

5. Conviction

It's hard to keep up with Michael Clague, both as an activist and as a cyclist. I have experience trying to do both. Michael has been an organizer, administrator, adult educator and consultant since the 1960s. Still going strong, he alternates between working for formal systems and grassroots groups. And he cycles at least eight thousand kilometres a year.

The eighteen-acre Britannia Community Services Centre in East Vancouver is one of Michael's many innovations. Britannia is an early example of a social innovation hub, bringing together schools and recreational services with social service agencies and community groups. It was conceived and designed in what we'd today call an open-source manner. Michael's work has garnered him an Order of Canada and the admiration of generations of activists.

What's most remarkable about innovators like Michael and the others you've met in this book isn't their achievements. It's the constancy of their convictions. Their ethics are not forged out of their experiences. Rather, their ethics have shaped their work. In his introduction to the Extraordinary Canadians book series, John Ralston Saul describes these eminent Canadians as sharing an "ethical cord strung taut through their work." His description fits the social innovators in this book too.

During a recent dinner with Vickie and me, Michael shared a couple of mishaps from his latest community organizing venture. "I don't take my strategies too seriously anymore," he laughed. "They come and go. Only my convictions have remained constant."

The social innovation journey is made up of tough choices. Powering through using the same brilliant strategy because it worked once before is not enough, especially if that strategy perpetuates animosities or widens the divide.

Michael is clearly a good strategist. Yet I wonder if the reason for his detachment from strategy is summed up in the famous Serenity Prayer: "God, grant me the serenity to accept the things I cannot change, / The courage to change the things I can, / And the wisdom to know the difference."

Lost Together: Letting Go and Hanging On at PLAN

Vickie and I were introduced to Dr. Frances Westley in 2004 at the beginning of our social innovation exploration. The three of us took an instant liking to each other. Frances became our adviser throughout the project and in many ways our guardian angel.

Because we stayed in touch afterwards, Frances knew that our hearts weren't in the day-to-day running of PLAN anymore. The two-year journey Vickie and I had taken only widened the gap between us and the rest of the PLAN family, who were content with the trajectory PLAN was on. We were exhilarated by the possibilities presented by what we were learning, but couldn't see how we could apply the emerging patterns and still manage our regular responsibilities at PLAN.

While Frances is a noted academic, she's also a champion pattern recognizer. When she's excited, words bubble out of her, floating around as aha moments for the rest of us to grab. Frances's academic achievements have been enlightened by what she learns from activists. She's equally at home with those on the front lines as with those in the academy. She's like a kid in a candy store with your stories. In return, she offers conceptual frameworks that bring clarity to your experiences. Frances is proof of psychologist Kurt Lewin's observation that there is nothing so practical as a good theory.

"It's not either/or," Frances said during one of our periodic meetings. "Every organization needs both explorers and conservers. The rest of PLAN is doing something very important, consolidating their hard-won efforts. You, on the other hand, want to explore other options. PLAN will become stronger by doing both. But *you* can't do both."

Ah, the irony of tasting your own medicine. Letting go was our mantra at PLAN. We had urged thousands of parents around the world to let go. It was the prerequisite to getting serious about planning for the future well-being of a son or daughter with a disability. Now Vickie and I were about to get an advanced lesson in letting go ourselves.

What we discovered was that fear is a natural reaction to moving closer to the truth, and that it's important to make friends with the unknown. It was liberating to accept that we are not in complete control and that being lost is a prerequisite to discovery. We no longer felt as helpless or hopeless. Instead, we became more alert, more aware and fully present. We learned that it's not about changing the world but about paying attention to how the world is changing. That's what *Getting to Maybe*, the book Frances co-wrote, is all about.

Emboldened by Frances's insight, Vickie and I found funding to hire new leaders for PLAN and stepped out of our day-to-day roles. The period of exploring "what's next?" eventually led to PLAN innovations like the RDSP and Tyze Personal Networks.

Here's how Frances and co-authors describe our fork-in-the-road experience:

> PLAN… scaled out its original innovation of creating support networks for children with disabilities, setting up networks for different families in numerous locations around the world. However, when it wanted to scale up its innovative thinking to a broader system about how society could provide long-term security for people with disabilities, the social innovation required different

tools and involved new legislation and new economic instruments, including the Registered Disabilities Savings Fund [sic].

Conclusion

Social innovation is enlightened by convictions. The guiding question becomes not whether we can solve our tough problems in time, but what is the right thing to do. It's our conviction that enables us to take risks, find our voices, trust our intuition – to act, regardless of what tomorrow may bring. "Who" is about personal responsibility, about seeing something that needs to be done and beginning.

While the light of inspiration and awareness strikes each of us individually, we are never alone. Others are waiting to join us. Rumi wrote: "Let the beauty of what you love be what you do. There are hundreds of ways to kneel and kiss the ground." The journey of mutual discovery and understanding has many paths and many practitioners.

If the answer to how is yes, and the answer to yes is you, then the answer to you is *us*.

Who Is as Important as How Means:
• Integrating your inner spiritual life with your outer activist one
• Paying attention to your personal blind spots
• Recognizing that every groove becomes a rut
• Acting on your convictions

JACK COLLINS: TRANSFORMER MAN

I'm trying to imagine what Jack Collins would say if he ever read this. He'd be uncomfortable for sure. There would be an awkward pause. He might stay silent or try to shift the conversation. A man of genuine authenticity, he always shunned the spotlight and was never one for what he would call small talk.

Sadly, Jack passed away a few days before I finished this book. I never got to show this story to him.

Jack had more reasons than most people to yield to despair, self-pity or bitterness. First he watched Helen, his wife, die painfully of cancer. His own cancer surgery followed. Then there was the loss of his beloved daughter, Pam, who was the reason Jack founded PLAN with Vickie and me. Finally, an insidious palsy appeared that became progressively worse. Jack had to give up driving as well as tennis, the game he loved.

Yet despite all this loss, Jack's heart continued to grow stronger, fuller and clearer.

Jack embodied the family arm of the disability movement. His steel-trap mind and warrior skills developed the advocacy apparatus that closed British Columbia's institutions for people with disabilities, and its segregated schools and sheltered workshops.

He was also PLAN's most precious resource. As founding president, he entered into the spirit of exploration. He was matter-of-fact about it. "New ideas take a lot of time to take hold," Jack would say. He enjoyed the back-and-forth and encouraged us to "talk and talk until we get it right."

Jack was a straight arrow, and parents knew it. I can't remember whether he spoke to three thousand families in our first five years, or five thousand families in our first three years. His credibility became PLAN's credibility. At one point PLAN had the largest membership base of all disability groups in the country.

Jack became an expert on special needs wills and trusts; he was sought after by both parents and lawyers. We estimate that his advice preserved $300 million in trust funds for the direct benefit of people with disabilities.

Above all, Jack was a truth teller. His blunt assessment of the inflexibility of the disability service system challenged many people. Some were a little afraid of him. Most were in awe.

When we celebrated PLAN's twentieth anniversary at Christ Church Cathedral in Vancouver, Jack walked to the front a little smaller than I remembered him. Although his hands on the podium shook, his voice was strong. He always had a kind of genius for speaking in simple tones and rhythms. He told us a humble story of a father's dreams for his daughter. He planted a vision of what's possible in each of us. He reminded us to never drift away from our dreams.

It was an intimate moment, and everyone knew it. To a person, we were electrified.

PADDLING TOGETHER

People are like trees, and groups of people are like forests.
While the forests are composed of many different kinds of trees,
these trees intertwine their roots so strongly that it is
impossible for the strongest winds which blow on our Islands to
uproot the forest, for each tree strengthens its neighbour, and their
roots are inextricably entwined.

In the same way the people of our Islands, composed of members
of nations and races from all over the world, are beginning to
intertwine their roots so strongly that no troubles will affect them.

Just as one tree standing alone would soon be destroyed by
the first strong wind which came along, so it is impossible for any
person, any family, or any community to stand alone against
the troubles of this world.

– Haida Chief Skidegate–Lewis Collinson

In 2006, as our two-year social innovation exploration was coming to an end, Vickie and I were invited on a sailing trip up the Inside Passage off the coast of British Columbia. Ian Gill, then head of Ecotrust Canada, arranged the trip. Ecotrust was helping the Haisla Nation repatriate a nine-metre mortuary pole stolen from the mouth of the Kitlope River in 1929.

As we entered Kitimat Inlet, indigenous elder Cecil Paul of the Haisla First Nation joined us. He had played a leading role in protecting the old-growth forests of his nation's territory, the Kitlope Valley, in the 1990s. He had also helped locate the missing mortuary pole, whose whereabouts were unknown for nearly seventy years.

The pole had a tangled history. With the assent of the Canadian government, it was sent in the 1920s to Sweden, where it was eventually discovered in the basement of a Stockholm museum. When Cecil Paul and other community leaders decided to bring the pole home, they faced funding barriers, policy obstacles, government negotiations (the pole was considered *Swedish* state property) and prejudice (the museum didn't think the Haisla people would take proper care of their own pole). There were also conflicting views within the Haisla community about making this project a priority, given the nation's many challenges.

When Vickie asked Cecil Paul how the community leaders had reconciled these divergent interests and sustained themselves for the long and complicated journey, he answered, "We built a spirit canoe. In a spirit canoe there is always room for one more."

****

I like the enabling metaphor of the canoe. The CBC's Peter Mansbridge once commented that it's hard to imagine Canada without the canoe. Its presence in every region of our country, from birchbark canoes in the east to kayaks in the north to dugout cedar canoes on the west coast, defines us as Canadians. This elegant vessel helped establish networks of travel, commerce and cultural exchange long before we became a country. Haida artist Bill Reid's sculpture of the Jade Canoe is a fitting testimony to its cultural significance. It was featured on the back of Canadian twenty-dollar bills issued between 2004 and 2012 and on a Canadian postage stamp. It's also on display outside the Canadian embassy in Washington, the international terminal of Vancouver's airport and the Canadian Museum of History.

The canoe that carries us along our social innovation journey holds a variety of occupants who are not always in agreement yet who are interdependent.

Each of us can imagine for ourselves who is on board. Many passengers are not of our choosing. They include people we're suspicious of or don't like. Who, we are certain, have created the perilous conditions for our journey. Who are oblivious to the challenges we face. Who aren't pulling their weight. Yet in order not to capsize in stormy seas, we must paddle in harmony. Spelling each other off when we get tired. Sharing our resources. Surviving – despite, or because of, our differences.

In this book's opening chapter I suggested that social innovation spreads when we become wise travellers. We've tried going it alone for too long. While each of the six patterns I've described gives you an opportunity to shift your mindset and try doing things another way, all six are connected by one warm line – they require us to paddle together.

The capacity for cooperation is embedded in human nature. And it is certainly embedded in Canada's nature.

John Ralston Saul describes Canada as a Métis civilization: a blend of First Nations and European influences. "What we are today has been inspired as much by four centuries of life with the indigenous civilizations as by four centuries of immigration," he writes in *A Fair Country*. Early fur traders and settlers would not have survived our wild terrain and harsh climate without support from Aboriginal people. John reminds us that Canada emerged from the indigenous idea of egalitarianism and of society as "an inclusive circle that expands and gradually adapts as new people join us."

The canoe was not only the most practical vessel to negotiate our vast land. It symbolizes a way of living together. Saul links Canada's commitment to peacemaking, medicare and multiculturalism to First Nations influence. Mutual dependence and partnerships are components of Canada's DNA, even though European settlers often failed to live up to these commitments – sometimes tragically so.

****

The quote that opens this chapter is from a former chief of the Haida Gwaii community of Skidegate. If anyone had a reason for not trusting in our interdependence, Chief Lewis Collinson did. Europeans decimated his nation. At the time of contact, the Haida population was in the tens of thousands. That number fell to less than five hundred by the early 1900s. The majority of people died of diseases such as smallpox and tuberculosis that were introduced by traders.

Today the Haida population has grown to twenty-five hundred. Haida culture is reviving. Its artists, poets and storytellers are known around the world. Children are learning their native language. Young adults eagerly train to become Haida Gwaii Watchmen, responsible for protecting cultural heritage in abandoned villages. A large chunk of the Haida archipelago is set aside as Gwaii Haanas, a national park reserve and Haida heritage site that the Haida Nation co-manages with the federal government.

This remarkable recovery is due to many factors, but surely one is the mindset reflected in Chief Lewis Collinson's remarks.

The wisdom of his words was palpable on July 1, 2006, when after a day-long celebration with fifteen hundred others, Vickie and I watched the youngest members of the Haisla community unveil their lost mortuary pole. A shiver went through the crowd. A vital piece of Haisla culture had been reclaimed, and the future of the nation's children seemed brighter.

For non-Aboriginal attendees it was a lesson in remembering because Canadians have a heritage of taking care of each other, of working together and of demonstrating ingenuity in the face of adversity.

****

Neil Young was once asked the source of his creativity. His answer was, as usual, enigmatic: "It's like Schubert said, I don't make up my music, I remember it."

In the same way, perhaps we don't have to "make" social innovation so much as remember it – remembering that we are all pulling together, wise travellers in the same spirit canoe.

NOTES, LINKS AND FURTHER
REFERENCES

Introduction

19 William Gibson
www.williamgibsonbooks.com

19 Geoff Mulgan, Simon Tucker & Nick Wilkie, *Social Silicon Valleys, A Manifesto for Social Innovation – What it is, Why it Matters, How it Can be Accelerated*, 2006
www.youngfoundation.org

20 Muhammad Yunus
www.pbs.org/opb/thenewheroes/meet/yunus.html

23 Tim Brodhead, *In a World of Unpredictable Change, What Canada Needs Most is RESILIENCE*, The J.W. McConnell Foundation, 2011
www.mcconnellfoundation.ca

26 Gregory Bateson as quoted in Bernard Poerksen & Hanne Detel, *The Unleashed Scandal – The End of Control in the Digital Age*, Imprint Academic, 2014

26 Francis Westley, Brenda Zimmerman & Michael Quinn Patton, *Getting to Maybe: How the World Is Changed*, Vintage Canada, 2007

Introduction: Further References

An Ecology of Mind is a film portrait of Gregory Bateson, celebrated anthropologist, philosopher, author, naturalist, systems theorist, and filmmaker, produced and directed by his daughter, Nora Bateson.
www.anecologyofmind.com

Alison Mathie & Gordon Cunningham (Eds.), *From clients to citizens: Communities changing the course of their own development*, Practical Action Publishing, 2008

Al Etmanski, *A Good Life*, Orwell Cove and Planned Lifetime Advocacy Network, 2004

Al Etmanski, *Safe and Secure – Seven Steps on the Path to a Good Life for People With Disabilities*, Planned Lifetime Advocacy Network, 2014

Asset Building for Social Change – Pathways to Large Scale Impact, Ford Foundation
www.fordfoundation.org

Wise Travellers

33   Skaay, as quoted in Robert Brighurst's book, *A Story as Sharp as a Knife: The Classial Haida Mythtellers and Their World*, Douglas & McIntyre, 2011

36   Wade Davis, *The Sacred Headwaters*, Greystone Books/David Suzuki Foundation, 2011

36   Charlie Leadbeater's excellent article *The Pro-Am Revolution* inspired my concept of the passionate amateur.
www.charlesleadbeater.net

36   Charles Leadbeater TED Talk entitled, The Rise of the Amateur-Professional.
www.ted.com

37   Angeles Arrien, Ph.D., *The Four-Fold Way: Walking the Paths of the Warrior, Teacher, Healer and Visionary*, HarperSanFrancisco, 1993

39   John McKnight & Peter Block, *The Abundant Community: Awakening the Power of Families and Neighborhoods*, Berrett-Koehler, 2010

41   Michele-Lee Moore & Francis Westley. 2011. Surmountable chasms: networks and social innovation for resilient systems. *Ecology and Society* 16(1): 5.
www.ecologyandsociety.org/vol16/iss1/art5/

43   "Tarot" by Shane Koyczan. Shane is an award-winning Canadian poet, author and performer
www.shanekoyczan.com

44   For further details on the Registered Disability Savings Plan see www.rdsp.com

Wise Travellers: Further References

Alan Broadbent, Chair of Maytree Foundation
www.maytree.com

Sherri Torjman and Caledon Institute of Social Policy
www.caledoninst.org

Clayton M. Christensen, Heiner Baumann, Rudy Ruggles & Thomas M. Sadtler. Disruptive Innovation for Social Change. *Harvard Business Review*, December, 2006

Katharine A. Pearson, *Accelerating our Impact: Philanthropy, Innovation and Social Change*, McConnell Foundation, 2007

Paul Hawken, *Blessed Unrest – How the Largest Social Movement in History Is Restoring Grace, Justice, and Beauty to the World*, Penguin Group, 2007

Pattern One: Think and Act Like a Movement

45   The member of The Tragically Hip are Gord Downie, Paul Langlois, Rob Baker, Gord Sinclair & Johnny Fay
www.thehip.com

46   The Womanly Art of Breastfeeding
www.llli.org

49   The Revolution Is Love with Charles Eisenstein
www.youtube.com/watch?v=BRtc-k6dhgs

49   Troy Duster as quoted in Michael Pollan's *New York Review of Books* article The Food Movement Rising
www.michaelpollan.com/articles-archive/the-food-movement-rising/

51   John McKnight on social movements vimeo.com/72047291

51   Brenda Zimmerman tamarackcommunity.ca/ssi8.html

52   Corby Kummer, *The Pleasures of Slow Food – Celebrating Authentic Traditions, Flavors, and Recipes*, Chronicle Books, 2002

52   Judith Marcuse and Centre for Art and Social Change
     www.icasc.ca

53   Bud L. Hall. 2009. A River of Life: Learning and Environmental Social Movements. *Interface* 1(1):46-78
     www.interfacejournal

53   Catherine Etmanski
     www.royalroads.ca/people/catherine-etmanski

53   Edward Burtynsky
     www.edwardburtynsky.com

53   Dr. Jan Christilaw and Vancouver Women's Hospital
     www.bcwomensfoundation.org

57   Ashoka Canada
     www.canada.ashoka.org

59   www.sharktruth.com

Pattern One — Further References

The Asset-Based Community Development Institute (ABCD)
www.abcdinstitute.org

www.idlenomore.ca

John McKnight, *The Careless Society: Community And Its Counterfeits*, Basic Books, 1995

SIG interview with John McKnight
www.sigeneration.ca/starting-small-john-mcknight-community-driven-change

Adam Hochschild, *Bury the Chains – Prophets and Rebels in the Fight to Free an Empire's Slaves,* Mariner Books, 2006

Marian Leonard Tompson, *Passionate Journey – My Unexpected Life,* Hale Publishing, 2011

John McKnight and Peter Block, *The Abundant Community: Awakening the Power of Families and Neighborhoods,* Berrett-Koehler, 2010
www.abundantcommunity.com

Brenda Zimmerman, Curt Lindberg & Paul Pisek, *Edgeware: Insights from Complexity Science for Health Care Leaders,* VHA, Inc., 1998

Charles Taylor, *Modern Social Imaginaries,* Duke University Press, 2004

Kalle Lasn, *Meme Wars – The Creative Destruction of Neoclassical Economics,* Seven Stories Press, 2012

Catherine Etmanski. 2012. Inch by Inch, Row by Row: Social Movement Learning on Three Oaks Organic Farm. In Budd L. Hall, Darlene E. Clover, Jim Crowther & Eurig Scandrett (Eds.), *Learning and education for a better world: The role of social movements,* Sense Publishers, 2012

Pattern Two: Create a Container for Your Content

61 Thomas King, *The Truth About Stories – A Native Narrative,* House of Anansi Press, 2003

62 Mike Harcourt, *Plan B – One Man's Journey from Tragedy to Triumph,* Mike Harcourt and John Lekich, John Wiley & Sons, 2006

63 Jan Zwicky, *Wisdom and Metaphor,* Brush Education Inc., 2014

64   Chen-Bo Zhong and Katie Liljenquist. 2006. Washing Away Your Sins: Threatened Morality and Physical Cleansing. *Science* Vol. 313 no. 5792 pp. 1451-1452

65   www.operationnezrouge.com

66   Sue Bookchin and Nancy Ross Be the Peace... Make A Change Project www.bethepeace.ca

67   Ola Tjornbo, Frances Westley & Darcy Riddell, *Case Study: The Great Bear Rainforest Story*, January, 2010 www.sig.uwaterloo.ca/highlight/case-study-the-great-bear-rainforest-story

68   Me to We co-founders Craig and Marc Kielburger www.metowe.com www.freethechildren.com

69   David Roche www.davidroche.com

69   Michael Jones, *The Soul of Place – Re-imagining Leadership Through Nature, Art and Community*, Friesen Press, 2014

70   Dan Yashinsky, *Suddenly They Heard Footsteps – Storytelling for the Twenty-first Century*, Vintage Canada, 2005 www.tellery.com/dan-yashinsky/

70   *To This Day* – Shane Koyczan www.tothisdayproject.com

70   Shane Koyczan, *To This Day – For the Bullied and Beautiful*, Annick Press, 2014

70   Upworthy www.upworthy.com

71   Tracey Friesen – Story Money Impact www.storymoneyimpact.com

72   Tyze
      www.Tyze.com
      Vickie Cammack & Kerry Byrne, Accelerating a Network
      Model of Care: Taking a Social Innovation to Scale,
      Technology Innovation Management Review, July, 2012
      www.timreview.ca/article/578

74   Diane Riley
      www.tinyurl.com/qb2htfz

75   InSite
      www.communityinsite.ca

75   Canadian Drug Policy Coalition
      www.drugpolicy.ca

Pattern Two: Further References

Michel Jones
www.thesoulofplace.com

For a video snapshot of the Great Bear Rainforest, see
filmmaker Bill Weaver's *Sound Venture* http://vimeo.
com/115492762

David Roche, *The Church of 80% Sincerity*, Perigee, 2008

The Perfect Flaw, a 2005 documentary about David Roche by
Mike Grundmann www.films.com/id/5554

George Lakoff, *Don't Think of An Elephant! Know Your Values
and Frame the Debate*, Chelsea Green Publishing Company,
2004

Susan Boyd, Donald MacPherson and Bud Osborn, *Raise
Shit! Social Action Saving Lives*, Fernwood Publishing, 2009

Donald MacPherson, A Framework for Action – A Four-
Pillar Approach to Drug Problems in Vancouver, April 24,
2001

Bruce K. Alexander, *The Globalization of Addiction, A study in Poverty of the Spirit*, Oxford University Press, 2008

Bonnie Sherr Klein's *Shameless: The ART of Disability*, a 2006 NFB feature
www.nfb.ca/film/shameless_the_art_of_disability/

Pattern 3: Set the Table for Allies, Adversaries and Strangers

77   Guy Vanderhaeghe, *A Good Man*, McClelland & Stewart, 2011

78   Paul Born, *Community Conversations, Mobilizing the Ideas, Skills, and Passion of Community Organizations, Governments, Businesses, and People*, BPS Books, 2012

78   Vibrant Communities Canada
www.vibrantcommunities.ca

80   Mark Kingwell, *The World We Want: Virtue, Vice and the Good Citizen*, Penguin, 2000

80   Social Innovation Generation
www.sigeneration.ca

80   For another perspective on the challenge of working together, see Stephen Huddart http://www.mcconnellfoundation.ca/news/on-the-co-evolution-of-innovation-and-evaluation-reflections-on-the-2014-evaluation-roundtable-2

81   Rosemary Sullivan, *By Heart: Elizabeth Smart/A Life*, Viking Penguin Group, 1991

83   Kate Sunderland, *Make Light Work in Groups - 10 Tools to Transform Meetings, Companies and Communities*, Incite Press, 2012

84   Mark Kingwell, p.116

84   Bill Drayton. 2006. Everyone is a Changemaker – Social
      Entrepreneurship's Ultimate Goal, *Innovations*, Winter: 3
      www.ashoka.org

84   John Ralston Saul
      www.johnralstonsaul.com

85   Peter Block, *Community: The Structure of Belonging*, Berrett-
      Koehler, 2009

86   Ashoka Changemakers
      www.changemakers.com

86   Delyse Sylvester
      www.beedie.sfu.ca/profiles/DelyseSylvester

86   SME Finance Challenge
      www.changemakers.com/SME-Finance

87   Peace Dividend Trust (since Renamed Building Markets)
      www.buildingmarkets.org

88   Jason Mogus and Communicopia
      www.communicopia.com

88   Web of Change
      www.webofchange.com

89   Social Innovation Labs
      www.sigeneration.ca/home/labs

91   Philia A dialogue on caring citizenship
      www.philia.plan.ca/

91   Centre for Inclusion and Citizenship at the University of
      British Columbia
      www.cic.arts.ubc.ca

92   Andrew Cohen, *Lester B. Pearson*, Penguin Group, 2008

93   Together: Respecting Our Future
      www.tinyurl.com/mpca5ue

93   BC Social Innovation Council – BC Partners for Social
     Impact
     www.hubcapbc.ca

Pattern Three — Further References

Paul Born, *Deepening Community – Finding Joy Together in
Chaotic Times*, Berrett-Koehler, 2014

Community Conversations by Paul Born, BPS Books, 2012

Adam Kahane, *Power and Love*, Berrett-Koehler, 2009

Pattern 4: Mobilize Your Economic Power

95   Rev. Dr. Moses Coady
     www.coady.stfx.ca

97   Stewards of Affordable Housing for the Future
     www.sahfnet.org

98   Disposable Income Statistics
     Abilities Magazine, Fall 2013
     www.abilities.ca

99   Boomer demographic. Twitter reference.
     www.tinyurl.com/kpb7zt8

100 Pink tourism (Kinsey survey)
     www.wildemarketing.com/pink_dollars.html

100 Toronto Pride
     www.tinyurl.com/nhayfg4

104 Entrepreneurial income 35% and rising (Boston Consulting
     Group)
     http://tinyurl.com/khrzdcb

104 Nicole Rycroft
     www.Canopyplanet.org

105 Ron Layton and Light Years IP
www.lightyearsip.net

106 Vancouver Tool Library
www.vancouvertoollibrary.com

106 Mark Anielski
www.anielski.com

107 Cities for People
www.citiesforpeople.ca

108 Coro Strandberg
www.corostrandberg.com

108 Centre for Social Innovation and Impact Investing at UBC
Sauder School of Business
www.sauder.ubc.ca

109 Muhammad Yunus, *Building Social Business – The New Kind of Capitalism That Serves Humanity's Most Pressing Needs*, PublicAffairs, 2010

113 Marguerite Mendell and Nancy Neamtan (2010) The Social Economy in Quebec: Towards a New Political Economy, in *Researching the Social Economy*, Laurie Mook, Jack Quarter and Sherida Ryan (Eds.)

113 Marguerite Mendell. Financing the Social Economy in Quebec – A Work in Progress. *Making Waves*, Vol. 20, no. 3
www.base.socioeco.org/docs/mw200346.pdf

Pattern 4: Further References

Mark Anielski, *The Economics of Happiness*, New Society Publishers, 2007

Cities and Sharing Economy
www.tinyurl.com/nb3hwn9

John Restakis, *Humanizing the Economy – Co-operatives in the Age of Capital*, New Society Publishers, 2010

Marjorie Kelly, *Owning Our Future: The Emerging Ownership Revolution*, Berrett-Koehler, 2012

David Bornstein, *How to Change the World – Social Entrepreneurs and the Power of New Ideas*, Oxford University Press, 2004

Michael Lewis and Pat Conaty, *The Resilience Imperative – Cooperative Transitions to a Steady-State Economy*, New Society Publishers, 2012

Michael J. Sandel, *What Money Can't Buy – The Moral Limits of Markets*, Farrar, Straus and Giroux, 2012

Pattern Five: Advocate With Empathy

115 Mark Kingwell, p.19

116 Sean Moore
www.seanmoore.ca

117 Jane Jacobs, *Systems of Survival – A Dialogue on the Moral Foundations of Commerce and Politics*, Vintage, 1994

125 David Mitchell, Don't write off the public service yet, Contributed to *The Globe and Mail*, published Wednesday, June 22, 2011

126 Sheila Fraser, Auditor General of Canada, May 25, 2011

128 Mark Jaccard, The Accidental Activist – How an energy economist and former government advisor found himself blocking a coal train, *The Walrus Magazine*, March, 2013

129 The Right Honourable Joseph Clark at the 25th Annual Testimonial Dinner, Public Policy Forum, May 3, 2012

Pattern 5: Further References

Geoff Mulgan, *The Art of Public Strategy – Mobilizing Power and Knowledge For the Common Good*, Oxford, 2009

Sean Moore's Advocacy School
www.advocacyschool.org/

Max Bell Foundation Public Policy Training Institute
www.maxbell.org

Maytree Foundation Public Policy Training Institute
www.maytree.com

Pattern Six: Who Is as Important as How

133   John Mighton *The Varsity*, January 29, 2007
      www.tinyurl.com/n8fqtwh

135   Bill Gale and the Business Community Anti-Poverty
      Initiative
      www.bcapi.ca

136   Peter Block, *The Answer to How is Yes – Acting on What Matters,* Berrett-Koehler, 2003

137   Bill McKibben, Movements Without Leaders, *UNTE Reader*, August 21, 2013

137   Jacques Dufresne
      www.agora.qc.ca
      www.appartenance-belonging.org

138   Jean Vanier, *Community and Growth*, Paulist Press, 2002

139   Margaret Heffernan, *Willful Blindness – How We Ignore the Obvious at Our Peril*, Walker & Company, 2012

140   Darcy Riddell et al., Agency and Innovation in a Phase
      of Turbulent Change: Conservation in the Great Bear

Rainforest, in *Using a Positive Lens to Explore Social Change and Organizations,* Edited by Karen Golden-Biddle & Jane E. Dutton, Routledge, 2012

140   Shari Graydon, (Ed.), *I Feel Great About My Hands – And Other Unexpected Joys of Aging,* Douglas and McIntyre, 2011
www.sharigraydon.com
www.informedopinions.org

141   Robert A. Heinlein, *Stranger in a Strange Land,* G.P. Putnam's Sons, 1961

141   Alexandra Samuel and Rob Cottingham
Social Signal
www.socialsignal.com

142   John Mighton JUMP Math
www.jumpmath.org

142   John Mighton, *Half Life,* Playwrights Canada Press, 2005

142   Malcolm Gladwell, *Outliers – The Story of Success,* Back Bay Books, 2011

142   John Mighton, *The End of Ignorance,* Vintage Canada, 2008

143   John Ralston Saul, General Editor, *Penguin Extraordinary Canadians Series*
www.penguinrandomhouse.ca/programs/extraordinary-canadians

144   Dr. Frances Westley quote
www.ecologyandsociety.org/vol16/iss1/art5

147   Jack Collins speaking at PLAN's 20th Anniversary.
http://vimeo.com/9665693

Pattern 6: Further References

Ted Kuntz, *Peace Begins With Me*, 2005
www.peacebeginswithme.ca

Michael Clague, *Staying True, Staying the Course – Lessons From 10 Successful Community Service Organizations in British Columbia*, 1997-2008

Lance Gunderson & C.S. Holling (Eds.), *Panarchy – Understanding Transformations in Human and Natural Systems.* Island Press, 2002

Donna Thomson, *The Four Walls of My Freedom*, McArthur and Company, 2010

Paddling Together

149   Haida Chief Skidegate – Lewis Collinson
www.haidaheritagecentre.com

150   Ecotrust Canada
www.ecotrust.ca

151   John Ralston Saul, *A Fair Country – Telling Truths About Canada*, Penguin Canada, 2009

153   "It's like Schubert said" – Neil Young
www.tinyurl.com/kjzqam3

Paddling Together: Further References

Ian Gill, *All That We Say Is Ours – Guujaaw and the Reawakening of the Haida Nation*, Douglas and McIntyre, 2009

Totem: The Return of the G'psgolox Pole
http://www.nfb.ca/film/totem_the_return_of_the_gpsgolox_pole/

Sanford Osler, *Canoe Crossings – Understanding the Craft that Helped Shape British Columbia*, Heritage House, 2014

THANKS

To the people profiled in this book, particularly Marian Tompson, Mike Harcourt, Paul Born, Bill Kelly, Sean Moore and Bill Gale.

To my Social Innovation Generation (SiG) companions Allyson Hewitt, Cheryl Rose, Devon Krainer, Frances Westley, Geraldine Cahill, Ilse Treurnich, Kelsey Spitz, Meena Nallainathan, Stephen Huddart, Tim Brodhead, Tim Draimin and the late Katherine Pearson and Brenda Zimmerman.

To BC Partners for Social Impact, particularly Gord Hogg, Jim Fletcher, Ken Gauthier, Molly Harrington, Trish Sterloff, Colleen McCormick, Rachel Holmes and Shelley McNellis.

To Peter and Nancy Mortifee for their hospitality and Mary Schendlinger, Patty Osborne, Adam Kahane, Paul Born and Sandra Shields for their advice and referrals.

To Catherine Etmanski, Cheryl Rose, Donna Thomson, Molly Harrington, Steve Piersanti of Berrett-Koehler, Vickie Cammack, Ted Kuntz and Tracey Friesen for clarifying ideas and reviewing various drafts of the manuscript.

To editors Shari Graydon, Barbara Pulling and Francis Peck for culling, restructuring and polishing. And my long-standing editorial companion Linda McDaniel, who is so much more than an editor.

To Sara Bailey for her beautiful design, Cindy Hughes for her photo and Kris Klaasen and Teresa Gustafson for producing another good-looking book for me.

To Canadian songwriters for their music and lyrics many of which insinuated their way into the book.

To Severn Cullis-Suzuki for the Foreword.

To Jason Mogus for his kindness and strategic advice.

To Lisa Joy Trick for embracing with gusto the task of spreading the word and for bringing her daughter Xandie to our meetings.

And to Vickie, my precious companion.

Thanks to our distribution partners:

Notes:

Notes:

Notes:

Notes: